THE ELEMENTS OF TAOISM

Martin Palmer is director of the International Consultancy on Religion, Education and Culture (ICOREC). He has been a student of Chinese since the early 1970s when he went to work in Hong Kong. He is the author and editor of many books on Chinese folk religion as well as a translator of Chinese classical texts. He studied Theology, Religious Studies and Chinese at Cambridge and his favourite pastime is cooking Chinese food.

The *Elements Of* is a series designed to present high quality introductions to a broad range of essential subjects.

The books are commissioned specifically from experts in their fields. They provide readable and often unique views of the various topics covered, and are therefore of interest both to those who have some knowledge of the subject, as well as those who are approaching it for the first time.

Many of these concise yet comprehensive books have practical suggestions and exercises which allow personal experience as well as theoretical understanding, and offer a valuable source of information on many important themes.

In the same series

The Aborigine Tradition
Alchemy
The Arthurian Tradition
Astrology
The Bahá'í Faith
Buddhism
Celtic Christianity
The Celtic Tradition
The Chakras
Christian Symbolism
Creation Myth
Dreamwork
The Druid Tradition
Earth Mysteries
The Egyptian Wisdom
Feng Shui
Gnosticism
The Goddess
The Grail Tradition
Graphology
Handreading
Herbalism
Hinduism

Human Potential
The I Ching
Islam
Judaism
Meditation
Mysticism
Native American Traditions
Natural Magic
Numerology
Pendulum Dowsing
Prophecy
Psychosynthesis
The Qabalah
Reincarnation
The Runes
Shamanism
Sufism
Tai Chi
The Tarot
Visualisation
Yoga
Zen

> **the elements of**

taoism
martin palmer

Shaftesbury, Dorset • Rockport, Massachusetts • Brisbane, Queensland

First published in Great Britain in 1991 by
Element Books Limited
Shaftesbury, Dorset SP7 8BP

Published in the USA in 1991 by
Element Books, Inc.
PO Box 830, Rockport, MA 01966

Published in Australia in 1991 by
Element Books Limited
for Jacaranda Wiley Limited
33 Park Road, Milton, Brisbane 4064

Reprinted 1993
Reprinted 1994
Reprinted 1995
Reprinted 1996

This edition 1996

Cover design by Max Fairbrother
Illustrations by Pauline Howcroft
Typeset by Selectmove Ltd, London
Printed and bound in Great Britain by
Biddles Limited, Guildford and King's Lynn

British Library Cataloguing in Publication
data available

Library of Congress Cataloging in Publication
data available

ISBN 1–86204–040–0

Dedicated, with love and thanks
to Janet Fischer, for all that she
has brought into my life and for
all that is to come.

Completed 3-4-01

CONTENTS

1 · THE WAY OF THE TAO

'In a back lane a sage quietly lived a simple life,
having just enough food to keep himself alive.
Poor and miserable though he might seem,
yet he felt happy and held himself in high esteem.'

This text, divination number 63 from the fortune-telling poems of
the immortal Wong Tai Sin, captures the essence of the Taoist sage.
Outwardly nothing, all is within. Scorning what the world considers
valuable, the Taoist sage looks within and finds the whole cosmos
and the purpose of life. Looking outward, the sage sees a world
riven with striving.

This image of the reclusive sage is very powerful in Taoism, as is
the idea of immortality. The Taoist idea of immortality is not just
a spiritual concept. Immortality consists of transforming the whole
body into an eternal vehicle for the soul.

Taoism is not an easy faith or philosophy to understand. The
opening verse of the *Tao Te Ching*, the great classic of early Taoism
(fifth to fourth century BC) makes this clear.

'The Tao that can be spoken of is not the real Tao.
The name that can be named is not the true name.'

(*Tao Te Ching*, Chapter 1.)

1

Chuang Tzu, the fourth century BC writer, put it equally explicitly:

> 'The Great Tao is not named;
> Great Discriminations are not spoken;
> Great Benevolence is not benevolent;
> Great Modesty is not humble;
> Great Daring does not attack.
> If the Tao is made clear it is not the Tao.'

(*Chuang Tzu*, Chapter 2.)

The Taoist sage could expect to spend years and years studying before any glimmering of understanding reached him. Wong Tai Sin, quoted above, spent forty years in seclusion studying and perfecting his understanding. It was a hard path to walk, but Lieh Tzu, one of the three greatest writers of early Taoism (c. third century BC) puts this struggle in context.

'Yang Chu said; The longest life is but a hundred years and not one man in a thousand lives to that age. Suppose there is one who does. Half of that time is occupied with infancy and senility. Of the other half, almost half is wasted in sleeping at night and naps during the day time. And almost half is lost in pain, illness, sorrow, grief, death and deaths in the family. I would estimate that in the ten years or more (that is left to him), a man has hardly an hour in which he is quite content and free from constant worry. Then what is the purpose of life? Life is only for the enjoyment of beauty and wealth, sound and colour. But beauty and wealth cannot always be indulged in. . . . Fame causes us to advance and the law forces us to retreat. Nervously we struggle for the hollow praise of the moment and try to arrange things so as to extend our glory after our death. In gingerly fashion we exercise the utmost caution over what we hear with our ears and what we see with our eyes. We grieve over the right and wrong of our body and mind. Thus we do but miss the perfect happiness of the years as they go by and cannot give ourselves free rein even for an hour. What is the difference between this and being doubly chained inside an inner prison?'

(*Lieh Tzu*, 7:1b.)

2

To see how the sages of Taoism answered the question of the purpose of life, we need to go back beyond the sages to the cosmology of the Tao.

THE ETERNAL ULTIMATE

In Chapter 42 of the *Tao Te Ching*, we are told that the Tao is the origin of everything. This is expressed thus:

> The Tao gives birth to the One;
> The One gives birth to the Two;
> The Two give birth to the Three;
> The Three give birth to all things.

Tao is often called 'The Way' in translation. This does not really do justice to its cosmological depth of meaning. In its manifestation through the words of sages such as Lao Tzu (the *Tao Te Ching*), Chuang Tzu (his book is named after him) or Lieh Tzu (likewise), through the path trodden by the sages and immortals and so forth, it is indeed a Way, a Path. But Taoism teaches that it is more than that. Tao is the ultimate source of all, the origin before origin and the uncreated which creates everything. The *Tao Te Ching* spells this out clearly. Chapter 32 talks of the Tao as being forever indefinable. It is the power beyond power and it flows through the world, like a river heading to the sea, back to its origin. Chuang Tzu says:

> 'The Tao has reality and evidence, but no action and no form. It may be transmitted but cannot be received. It may be attained but cannot be seen. It exists in and through itself. It existed before Heaven and Earth, and indeed for all eternity. It caused the gods to be divine and the world to be produced.'
>
> (*Chuang Tzu*, Chapter 6.)

For Taoists, the Tao is the eternal ultimate, beyond even Unity and Oneness. As such, it is also beyond language, a point which Chuang Tzu makes time and time again in his writings. Thus we should turn from these attempts to express the inexpressible, to its more visible aspects, the Unity and interrelatedness of all life and the Way by which Tao moves and creates both the material and spiritual worlds.

What we have to discard is the concept that Tao is in any sense a creator god. In later Taoism, the Three Pure Ones of Taoism came to symbolize the personification of these Taoist principles, but were intended to point the way rather than be Creators (see pages 114–5). The Tao creates simply because it is the actual essence of all things. It does not set out to 'create' but things emerge as a result of Tao. It is what the *Tao Te Ching* refers to as the 'natural way'. The great Taoist commentator of the third to fourth centuries AD, Kuo Hsiang, put it thus:

'But let us ask whether there is a Creator or not. If not, how can he create things? If there is, he is capable of materializing all the forms. Therefore before we can talk about creation, we must understand the fact that all forms materialize by themselves. If we go through the entire realm of existence, we shall see that there is nothing, not even the penumbra, that does not transform itself beyond the phenomenal world. Hence everything creates itself without the direction of any Creator. Since things create themselves, they are unconditioned. This is the norm of the universe.'

(Commentary on Chuang Tzu, sec. 2, 2:46–47 – quoted in Bary, *Sources of Chinese Tradition*.)

In the liturgical text of the 'Ling-pao Five Talismans', this description of the essence of being is given in more detail. Describing the impact of the existence of the Way in the context of the sacred words created before all time, the text says:

'The visible world was generated.
The workings of water and fire,
Life and death,
The myriad kalpas, and
The light of primordial yang were initiated.
The two principles of yin and yang
Used them to carve out the three realms.
The holy sages mounted them,
To attain union with the transcendent.
The five sacred peaks hold them,
And are thereby filled with spiritual power.
All things possessing them have life breath (ch'i).'

(Wu-shang Pi-yao, Chapter 24, page 4b, line 3 – quoted in Saso, *The teachings of Taoist Master Chuang*.)

The above text illustrates the way in which the Tao moves all things

4

in their essence, but without purpose and intent. This is the famous concept of non-action (*wu-wei*, see pages 8–9). The unity of all in the Tao means that in any action which is natural, which occurs rather than is forced, the Tao is active. Putting it in human terms, the *Tao Te Ching* describes the perfect sage ruler as one who governs in such a way that the people are unaware that he governs them and simply believe that what happens is nature's way.

In acting naturally, by non-action, by just letting things be and following the Way, the ruler sage is in harmony with his own essence, the Tao beyond unity. Being in harmony, he is in unity and all his actions will thus express this unity and further it. This is the core of the idea that Tao gives birth to One.

'The One gives birth to the Two' concept has already been hinted at above in the quote from the *Wu-shang Pi-yao*. The Two are the twin forces of the yin and yang. These forces are complete opposites. Black and white; male and female; hot and cold – they represent within them all that is and can be, but in opposition. In their eternal struggle, which is the struggle of natural forces not gods, they generate the energy (ch'i) which fuels the creation and which causes all to come to birth. They are not forces of harmony as they are often presented in the West. They are locked in a life and death struggle which neither can win, for at the very moment that one reaches the highest point of its power, it gives way to the other. This is why the yin yang symbol shows the two forces curled round each other, with a dot of the other in the centre of each. Chuang Tzu expresses their role and action, and the consequences:

> 'Little Understanding said, "Within the four cardinal points and the six boundaries of space, how did the myriad things take their rise?" T'ai-Kung T'iao replied, "The Yin and Yang reflected on each other, covered each other and reacted with each other. The four seasons gave place to one another, produced one another and brought one another to an end."'
>
> (*Chuang Tzu*, Chapter 25, Legge's translation.)

All things have their origin in the interaction of the two opposites of yin and yang. But what of the concept 'Two gives birth to the Three'? This is the triad of Heaven, Earth and Humanity which is the form by which all living things come into actual existence. The link between them is set forth in cryptic form in Chapter 25 of the *Tao Te Ching*:

5

'The Tao is great;
Heaven is great;
Earth is great;
The King [representing humanity] is also great.
These are the four great powers of the universe.'

'Humanity follows the earth.
Earth follows Heaven.
Heaven follows the Tao.
Tao follows what is natural.'

Lieh Tzu puts is more expansively:

'Heaven and Earth cannot achieve everything;
The sage is not capable of everything;
None of the myriad things can be used for everything.

For this reason
It is the office of heaven to beget and to shelter,
The office of earth to shape and to support,
The office of the sage to teach and reform.
The office of each thing to perform its function.'

(*Lieh Tzu*, Chapter 1.)

Finally Taoism sees all living things as arising at the end of this cosmological progression. This is the meaning of the line, 'Three give birth to all living things'. Thus by going back, the Taoist arrives at the ultimate. This is indeed exactly what Taoist ritual does in the 'Liturgies of Cosmic Renewal' (see pages 125–7).

Now, it might seem as if we have completed the Taoist cosmology. However, there is one final insight which we need to have, for from it comes the whole Taoist approach to immortality, to medicine, to art and to what we are and the answer begins to emerge to the question, 'What is the purpose of life?'. Again let Chuang Tzu tell us:

'Heaven and Earth were born at the same time I was, and the ten thousand things [Chinese term for all living things] are one with me.'

(*Chuang Tzu*, Chapter 2.)

Because of the Tao, all things are linked. Thus we have within ourselves the microcosm of the universe. Thus is the interre-

6

latedness of all living things taken to its ultimate conclusion, that we are all each within each other. The fundamental unity of all in and through the Tao is what lies at the centre of Taoism, both in its earliest forms as well as in its development into more overtly religious beliefs and practices.

LANGUAGE AND MEANING

Before we turn to the Paths which Taoism has posited, we need to examine the problem of language and meaning in Taoism. Essentially Taoism at its heart denies the validity of language. Chuang Tzu has many examples of the inadequacy of both language and of knowledge. Here are two of the most famous of his comments.

> 'The Way cannot be thought of as being, nor can it be thought of as nonbeing. In calling it the Way we are only adopting a temporary expedient. . . . The perfection of the Way and things – neither words nor silence are worthy of expressing it. Not to talk, nor to be silent – this is the highest form of debate.'
>
> (*Chuang Tzu*, Chapter 25.)

> 'Once Chuang Chou [Chuang Tzu] dreamt he was a butterfly, a butterfly flitting and fluttering around, happy with himself and doing as he pleased. He didn't know he was Chuang Chou. Suddenly he woke up and there he was solid and unmistakable Chuang Chou. But he didn't know if he was Chuang Chou who had dreamt he was a butterfly, or a butterfly dreaming he was Chuang Chou.'
>
> (*Chuang Tzu*, Chapter 2.)

Because of this, Taoism, especially in its earliest forms as expressed by great books such as the *Tao Te Ching*, the *Chuang Tzu* or the *Lieh Tzu*, uses very cryptic terms and imagery. It is a mistake to take these literally (see pages 55ff). They are attempts to use both language and metaphor, whilst at the same time hinting that these are fundamentally inadequate. This is especially true in the *Chuang Tzu* and to a lesser extent in the *Lieh Tzu*. Here, humour and jokes are used to show how feeble the human mind is when it comes to understanding. Not many people associate Taoism with humour.

7

This is a great shame, for of all the world's many 'sacred texts', the *Chuang Tzu* is probably the funniest, most entertaining and at the same time one of the most stimulating. In particular Taoism uses paradox to make the reader think harder by the juxtaposition of extreme opposites. The *Tao Te Ching* does this to the point of making an art of it. Only fools would try to reconcile these opposites – the whole point is to revolutionize our ideas of what is definable and to open us up to new ideas and awarenesses of meaning. To miss this point is to fail to grasp the wonderful fun that Taoism has with language and imagery and thus to fall into a sort of Taoist fundamentalism. This sense of fun as a mode of teaching is perhaps best captured in the story of Liu Ling and his trousers (see page 107–8)!

SEEKING UNION

So, with all these ideas, images and cosmological concepts, what did the Taoist do as a result? The answer is complex and varied and constitutes a great proportion of the rest of this book. But in simplified form the answer is that the Taoist seeks to follow the Path or the Way of Tao and to achieve unity with the Ultimate Tao beyond the One. To do this Taoism has devised a vast array of methods and ways. These fall into the following broad categories.

WU-WEI

First of all there is the way of non-action – *wu-wei*. This is often represented as being the withdrawal of the Taoist from the wider world with all its temptations and illusions. This is what was referred to in the quote from Wong Tai Sin at the start of this chapter. It will be encountered time and time again in the stories of the sages. This withdrawal was certainly one response to the false path which the material world was taking. But it would be a great mistake to think that that was all there was to *wu-wei*. The greatest exponent of *wu-wei* is the *Tao Te Ching*. Yet this book is, in fact, a manual on how to govern the country, maintain law and order, run the army, organize farming and trade and so forth. *Wu-wei* is sometimes translated as non-selfishness. That is, the doing of things for entirely altruistic reasons. This is often a closer translation of what the *Tao Te Ching* means than the rather overly negative and totally passive sense of non-action. In many ways, Taoism is a very materialist faith, except that it sees the material as being subordinate to and ultimately controlled by the spiritual world. This ancient two world view arises from forces which were antique when Taoism first began and will be explored in the next chapter. In believing that this world can in fact be in harmony with the Tao, Taoism has a very specific interest in the world being run along proper lines. Indeed at times, Taoism has actually set up Taoist kingdoms in order to put these beliefs into practice (see pages 80ff).

The tension in Taoism is the challenge of how to run the world without acting from false interest. How can we truly rule in this way, in the way which the *Tao Te Ching* hopes for?

'I take no action and the people are reformed.
I enjoy peace and the people become honest.
I do nothing and people become rich.
I have no desires and the people return to the good and simple life.'

(*Tao Te Ching*, Chapter 57.)

This is what much of the *Tao Te Ching* then seeks to answer and what Taoists have sought to understand over the centuries.

THE PERSONAL QUEST FOR IMMORTALITY

The second response is that of the personal quest. This can best be described as the search for immortality. If we all come from and are the Tao, then surely we can actually become Tao and thus live for ever? Unlike much of western spirituality, Taoism sees the body as being necessary for immortality, not just the soul.

The quest for immortality involved two main approaches, one of introspection, that is meditation and reflection, often as part of the reclusive sage's lifestyle; the other involved attempts to change the body physically into an eternal form – alchemy.

In this quest for immortality, Taoism spawned literally hundreds of different groups who all sought different paths. Some of the main ones will be explored later in the book, as will the whole idea of immortality. For the present, let the great fourth century AD Taoist Ko Hung spell out just some of these.

9

'It is hoped that those who nourish life will learn extensively and comprehend the essential, gather whatever there is to see and choose the best. It is not sufficient to depend on cultivating only one thing. It is also dangerous for people who love life to rely on their own speciality. Those who know the techniques of the Classic of the Mysterious Lady and the Classic of the Plain Lady [books on sexual regimen] will say that only the "art of the chamber" will lead to salvation. Those who understand the method of breathing exercises will say that only the permeation of the vital power [ch'i] can prolong life. Those who know the method of stretching and bending will say that only physical exercise can prevent old age. And those who know the formulas of herbs will say that only medicine will make life unending. They fail in their pursuit of Tao because they are so onesided.'
(*Pao-p'u Tzu*, 6:4a – from Bary, *Sources of Chinese Tradition*.)

LITURGY AND RITUAL

A third way is via the use of liturgy and ritual. Many of the aims of the previous two models are also the aims of the liturgies, magic and rituals of so many of the schools of Taoism. The desire of the Taoists here is to become the channel and agent through which the world is kept in balance, evil forces are overcome and life is continued and improved – all through harnessing oneself to the forces of the cosmos, the forces emanating from the Tao. This might be as individualistic as using liturgy to restore a proper relationship to the Tao for a dead soul or it might be by seeking to channel the Tao into revitalizing the world. This is an example of the former:

'Take refuge in the Treasures of the Masters: they open the door to tranformation and to communication with Heaven; they are the mainstays of the Origin, the embodiment of the Way. It is the Golden Real One who developed the teaching and revealed the golden rituals which save from distress and deliver from ignorance. We beseech you to draw near, that we may share in the marvellous fruits of your teachings.'
(From Ofuchi's *Chugokujin no shukyo girei*, following Lagerwey's translation in *Taoist Ritual in Chinese Society and History*.)

MORALITY

A fourth way is that of morality. The second book which Taoism traditionally ascribes to Lao Tzu, the mysterious figure in early Taoism, is essentially nothing more nor less than a code of morality based upon the precepts of Taoism. The book, which is far more popular in Chinese society than the *Tao Te Ching*, is called the *T'ai Shang Kan Ying P'ien*, which translates as 'The Writings of the Exalted One [Lao Tzu's title] on Response and Retribution'. A few sentences from this text will illustrate what is meant:

'The Exalted One says:

Curses and blessings do not come through gates, but man himself invites their arrival.

The reward of good and evil is like the shadow accompanying a body, and so it is apparent that heaven and earth are possessed of crime-recording spirits. . . .

The right way leads forward; the wrong way backwards.

Do not proceed on an evil path.

Do not sin in secret.

Accumulate virtue, increase merit.'

(Translated by Paul Carus.)

In other words, Taoism's Paths are immensely varied, complex and fascinating and are far from summed up in just studying the sage or the recluse as we shall see.

Taoism is one of the world's greatest faiths. Its origins lie far back in pre-history. Its influence is being felt today in parts of the world and in disciplines which fifty years ago would never have even heard of Taoism. In everyday life amongst the Chinese it is powerfully at work. Its myths and legends are amongst some of the most profound, funniest and most moving in the world. Its philosophical writings inspire, its liturgies and rituals are awesome. Yet Taoism is barely known in the West. We have read the *Tao Te Ching* and think we know the Tao. I need hardly say what the *Tao Te Ching* would say of such superficial understanding or how rude Chuang Tzu would have been about that! It is a world which we need to explore and which is slowly opening up to us. Any faith

11

which has a collection of over four thousand books of sacred literature is going to be both daunting and time consuming. But the journey has begun and it is one of the most fascinating in the world.

2 · THE ORIGINS OF TAOISM

Most people's image of Taoism is that of the wise sage, or the immortal, up on the mountain, far from the trials and pursuits of life – the sort of image which we encountered so often in Chapter 1. Certainly the sage is one strand within the complex history of Taoism. Yet there is another strand which arguably is the more important. It is the strand which merged with the philosophical and sagacious, with the quest for immortality and longevity, to form what we know as Taoism. It is the strand which made Taoism arise from an academic, scholarly background and made it a popular mass religion. The roots of this strand lie far back in the pre-history of China. Its first discernible manifestation is through the strange worlds of the shamanist.

In Chapter 3 we shall turn to look at the strand of Taoism which emerged from the great philosophical teachings and musings of the wise men of China. We shall look at the roots of the concept of Tao itself and its role in both Confucianism and Taoism. But the simple fact is that Taoism as a living religion would probably never have developed were it not for the influences brought to bear by shamanism. At the time when the philosophical roots of Taoism began to emerge, there were, as the Chinese put it, 'A Hundred Schools' contending for the public's attention. Most have disappeared except as footnotes in history. It was the shamanistic dimension of Taoism which both gave it greater staying power and ultimately created Taoism as the folk religion of today.

SHAMANISM

Shamanism is the name given to what many have described as the world's first major religion. Starting some eight thousand years ago in Siberia, it spread down into China, across to Japan and into South East Asia. It travelled across the land-bridge from Siberia to Alaska and from there down the length of North and Central America. Its practitioners are still working to this day and it is from them as well as from some ancient sources that we know a little about this great religious tradition.

The core belief in shamanism is that there are two worlds which lie side by side, sometimes overlapping, but each distinct. These worlds are the physical one which we inhabit and the spiritual one which the forces which guide and control the physical world inhabit. As the 'lesser' world, we dwellers therein are to some extent at the mercy of the spiritual world. Its intrusion into our world can bring healing or it can bring sickness; good fortune or ill. The spirit world parallels all life on the physical plane – thus every tree, stream, animal or rock has its spirit. To harm or abuse these is to court disaster. It is therefore of considerable importance that we have some way of communicating with the spiritual world. This is where the shaman becomes crucial. He or she is able to enter into the spirit world and to communicate with the forces of the spirit world. This is done through a trance state during which the shaman speaks with or becomes the mouthpiece for the spirits.

The power and authority of such people is very considerable. In shamanistic cultures, no important decision is made without recourse to a shaman. When illness or hardship strikes, the shaman enters the spirit world to seek the cause of this distress and then tells the community what offence has caused this. In its perception of all the elements of the physical world being mirrored in the spiritual world, it teaches a very cautious and respectful attitude to nature. It seeks, to use a Taoist phrase, to ensure that the people follow the Way of Nature and abide by its powers and rights. In its very model of two worlds, it lays the ground for the concept of there being a

14

Natural Law, a Way which is to be followed in the material world if distress and disaster are not to arise.

The word shaman comes from the Tungus people of Siberia. Their traditional homeland is close to the furthest northern borders of the Chinese world. There is no doubt that from an early age, shamanistic influences spread down into China. While all physical evidence of such a spread has disappeared – or possibly yet remains to be discovered – we can see the influence in the earliest myths of China. These are the great myths which are still told by Taoists to this day.

FU HSI

According to the myths, the first 'ruler' of China was Fu Hsi. In all the legends it is to him that the spirits reveal how to bring human beings to civilization. It is Fu Hsi who reveals to humans how to calculate the agricultural calendar; how to farm and practise agriculture; how to form the institutions of marriage and government. To him is credited the invention of writing. He is also the one who invented the eight trigrams, as the Great Treatise in the *I Ching* tells us:

> 'When in ancient times Fu Hsi ruled the world, he looked up to observe the phenomena of the heavens, and gazed down to observe the contours of the earth. He observed the markings of birds and beasts and how they adapted to their habitats. Some ideas he took from his own body, and went beyond this to take other ideas from other things. Thus he invented the eight trigrams in order to comprehend the virtues of spiritual beings and represent the conditions of all things in creation.'

The best description of how and why a shamanist functions is that by studying and knowing nature, he or she is able to reach out to nature. Through this understanding the shamanist can then communicate with the spirit world and have revealed to him or her, the truth of life. In the legends of Fu Hsi we can see a powerful shamanist portrayed, almost a founder-figure shamanist. This is given further credence by a facet of the stories of Fu Hsi which later writers (post-Confucius, c. fifth century BC) gloss over or leave out altogether.

What was not often mentioned was that Fu Hsi was no ordinary human being. In the most ancient texts, he was described as being part human, part animal, as was his successor, Nua Kua, and the

15

third of these early rulers, Shen-nung. Fu Hsi's exact description is a matter of dispute. What is known is that Nua Kua had the head of a woman and the body of a snake and that she and Fu Hsi could join together by twining their tails! Shen-nung had the head of an ox.

What, you may be asking, does this indicate? It shows creatures who transcend the normal boundaries in the physical world by being both human and animal. As founder figures, ancestors, they sound remarkably similar to the Dreamtime figures in Australian Aboriginal mythology, who represent a linking of the spiritual life-giving world with the physical world.

The final stage in the evidence of some form of arcane memory of a powerful shamanistic background comes in the various skills which Fu Hsi, and after him Nua Kua and Shen-nung, taught human beings. These range from the skills attributed previously to Fu Hsi, through administration, iron smelting and casting attributed to Nua Kua, to medicine and ploughing attributed to Shen-nung. These wise rulers – reputed to have lived around 3000 BC – were able to teach the basic skills which gave human beings some power over their surroundings leading to the belief that such knowledge must have been given by the spirit world. In western culture we have a hint of this in the many legends associated with iron workers or smiths who were thought to be in touch with either good or bad spirits from whom they learnt their art.

THE FIVE AUGUST EMPERORS

After these three strange creatures, known as the Three August Ones, we come to the Five August Emperors. They were not only shamanists but were also the earliest manifestations of the political ruler. Indeed, by the time we get to the last two of these rulers, we have begun to lose sight of the shamanist and the ruler has become the dominant model.

The greatest of these Emperors, and the one most especially venerated by Taoists down the centuries, is the Yellow Emperor, Huang-ti. Legend places his rule around the period of 2500 BC and it is to him that many great inventions are attributed. He is credited with establishing the civil orders of the world – government in its best form. He is also the great explorer of medicine and one of the most famous and ancient of medical books in China is called 'The Pure Questions of the Yellow Emperor: The Classic of Internal

Medicine'. Written around the second century BC, it traces its teachings back to the Yellow Emperor.

The Yellow Emperor appears in many legends, but most of them involve his receiving secret or divine knowledge with which he overcomes various troubles. An example is given in the *Ch'i Men Tun Chia*. This book is a guide to warfare – the title translate as 'The Mysterious Gate for Hiding the Army' – based reputedly upon a book given to the Yellow Emperor.

The legend tells how a rebel, called Chih Yu had arisen with a formidable army. Chih Yu posed a serious threat to the Yellow Emperor and to the orderly world he had created. Huang-ti (the Yellow Emperor) set out to confront him, but the going was rough. While Huang-ti was on his travels, a goddess or spirit appeared to him and presented him with a book which gave him magical skills for warfare. This was no ordinary book, because its magic made it possible for Huang-ti to summon the wild animals, tigers, bears and other such creatures, to come and fight for him.

The mention of the bear in this text is quite significant. The bear is the oldest and most powerful of the forms which a shaman can take and represents the most awesome manifestation of the meeting of the spiritual with the physical world. Again, some commentators have seen this as further evidence of an almost submerged memory of the shamanistic background to Huang-ti. It certainly makes sense, given the later fascination and importance he has within Taoism.

By the time we get to the legends of the last two of the Five August Rulers, there is little evidence of their shamanist role. These rulers are the great heroes of the Confucians who have carefully removed anything which might make them supernatural in the old shamanistic Fu-Hsi mould. We shall encounter them again in the next chapter.

As stated earlier, at a philosophical or spiritual level, what shamanism had which helped the idea of Tao to emerge, was the sense of a relationship between the laws of nature and the ultimate power of the universe. This idea that harmony and balance within nature reflects the harmony and balance of the universe is as central to shamanism as it is to Taoism. Associated with this is the concept that change cannot be forced but only revealed or experienced. The shamanist is not in control of the spirits. They are in charge of him or her. Through the shaman they help humanity to repair any damage it has done and thus to return to the Way. The idea of flowing with the

17

Way, of bending and thus surviving, reflects the shamanistic attitude to life around us. One example of this attitude which lasted almost unaltered from the earliest times until the early twentieth century, was the role of the Emperor as mediator between Heaven, Earth and Humanity. In fulfilling this role, the Emperor acted out the role of the shamanist for the whole of his people. This is a classic example of shamanism and of the Taoist practice of following and being directed by the Way of Nature.

THE EMPEROR AS MEDIATOR

The Emperor and only the Emperor could act as the mediator between Heaven, Earth and the people. Each year he had to make sacrifices and offerings to appease the forces of nature which had been disturbed by human actions during the preceding year. In order to do this, the Emperor went into strict religious retreat, fasting for three days before the offerings could be made. He was quite literally isolated during this period. When he travelled from the palace to the Temple of Heaven, the streets were cleared and everyone was kept behind locked doors, so that nothing should distract the Intercessor from the task of offering sacrifices to make amends with his ancestors, with the Celestial Court and with Heaven itself. Beyond this, he was also there to ensure that at the most crucial point of the year, the winter solstice, the balance was maintained and the swing of yin to yang and vice versa was sustained. By offering his sacrifices and ensuring that Humanity, Heaven and Earth were in accord, the Emperor guaranteed that the yang principle should start to have the upper hand again, as the days moved away from the longest night towards the longest day. Only through the person of the Emperor, ritually prepared and functioning, could the spirit world and the material world be put together in perfect harmony and the round of rebirth and spring commence once more. The ruler exemplified the whole people, yet he was also above them.

In pre-Christian era times, the vast majority of the people of China found their identity in the clan or family and in the small states. They were firmly locked into a structure which gave them purpose, place and meaning. At the top of this, alone, stood the ruler. He was the figurehead, the one who could communicate with the spirits on behalf of everyone – just like the shamanist. Indeed, so strong is this

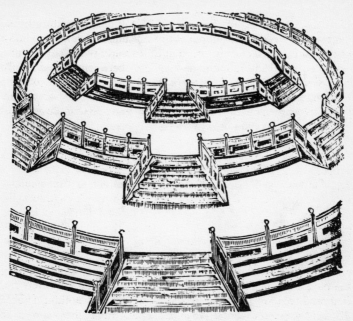

The Altar of Heaven, where the Emperor stood to represent Humanity

idea of the ruler alone being able to face the spirit world, alone at the top of a pyramid of relationships in which everyone had their place, that a common title for the Emperor was The Lonely Ruler.

These hints of the shamanist influence on the development of both kingship and of conceptual frameworks in ancient China provide us with an important thread leading to the rise of both a Taoist outlook on life and to the rise of religious Taoism. But there are also other strands within the prehistory of China which had an important influence on this process. Magic, exorcisms, divination, astrology and the calendar are a part of this – and in at least one area, we encounter echoes of the shamanist again.

THE FANG-SHIH

In the *Chou Li*, the Records of the Rites of the Chou Dynasty, in a text which may relate to the seventh century, we find a description of an official called the *fang-hsiang-shih*. This official was responsible for exorcisms and, in later descriptions of these *fang-shih*, they also delve into medicine, divination and other such practices. What is so interesting is the description of the ritual clothing. To perform his exorcisms, the *fang-hsiang-shih* wore a bearskin mask. Furthermore, the term *fang* comes from a term meaning people from the outlying areas of the country, such as the Siberian edges of the 'Empire'. Here we seem to have a clear reference to a shaman.

A fuller description of these *fang-shih* magicians was given by China's foremost historian of antiquity, Ssu-ma Ch'ien (145–90 BC). What he described could almost be an exact description of certain kinds of Taoists. Describing *fang-shih*, Ssu-ma Ch'ien wrote:

'Sung Wu-chi, Cheng-po Ch'iao, Chung Shang, Hsien-men Kao and Tsui Hou were all men of Yen who practised magic and followed the Way of the immortals, discarding their mortal forms and changing into spiritual beings by means of supernatural aid.'

Many of these activities – magic, astral travel and the pursuit of immortality – are the hallmarks of the Taoist sages and teachers. What is significant about the *fang-shih* is that they appear to mark a stage when the old shamanists from the outerlands, with their strange bear-related rituals, became socially acceptable within the new, more sophisticated courts of China, even if later the Confucians often despised them. As we shall see in Chapter 4, the *fang-shih* kept alive the old shamanist ideas and practices, modified them, and laid the foundations for the later rise of what is termed 'religious Taoism'. We also known that around the fourth century BC, shamanists were still very much part of the scene in the state of Chu, as evidenced in collections such as the 'Nine Songs' or 'Songs of the South' which date from that time.

RELIGION AND PHILOSOPHY

It is perhaps time to introduce the terms 'religious Taoism' and 'The School of Taoism'. In Chinese there are two phrases used to describe the very different ways in which Taoism developed. These terms are *Tao Chia* and *Tao Chiao*. *Tao Chia* refers to the School of Taoism, the philosophical aspect of the faith. This is exemplified by the writings of Lao Tzu, Chuang Tzu, Lieh Tzu and others. *Tao*

Chiao refers to the religion of Tao. This is the magical, divinational and popular manifestations of Taoism which we shall examine in Chapter 4. Both lay claim to the same founding figure, Lao Tzu, but as we shall see the differences of interpretation are considerable.

However, it is easy to be misled by these terms. Both are terms applied by others, by those who came after or those who stand outside the faith. As we shall see later, the writers of the _Lao Tzu_, _Chuang Tzu_, etc were not 'Taoists' – that is, they did not see themselves as belonging to a group so called. They drew upon traditions and ideas which were current at the time, ideas which were held in common with Confucians, with shamans, with practitioners of the cult of immortality. However, there gradually evolved over the centuries, a faith, described by its contemporaries as 'Taoism', in which the philosophical and the shamanistic, along with other influences, came together. We can, if we so wish, pick out the strand of Taoist philosophical thought. At times it does re-emerge, as in the renaissance of Taoist philosophical thought of the third and fourth centuries AD. But by then, even the most ardent Taoist philosophers were also engaged in other, less 'pure' aspects of Taoism, such as alchemy or physical exercises for longevity and immortality. So whilst it is useful to see that there was a school or philosophical tradition which helped to feed and create Taoism, it is not particularly helpful to see them as in opposition. Taoism is far more complex and fascinating than that. But let us return to the antecedents of the Taoist movement.

The shamanistic and _fang-shih_ dimension gave its greatest input into the creation of a popular Taoism, but the core shamanistic idea of being in relationship, in balance with Nature and the Spirit world, undoubtedly contributed to the philosophical idea of the Tao and of its being the basis of reality. Together these ideas helped the emergence of the full significance of the Way itself.

ASTROLOGY AND THE CALENDAR

There was another aspect of life in early China which also helped the development of the concept of the Way. That was astrology and the calendar.

At the heart of the Way is the notion that Humanity needs to be in accord with and flow with the Way. This means recognizing that we are but part of something much greater and more significant. It is in contradistinction to the western model of reality which posits God as the ultimate, but gives Humanity a nearest-to-God role in the universe. In the West, meaning is given to the rest of creation through human use of it. This is the reverse of the Chinese and especially the Taoist idea. One of the roots of the Chinese idea lies in the ancient craft of astrology and calendar-making. Both activities are concerned with observing the Way of the universe and of Nature and with tailoring human behaviour and expectations to fit within that grander overall pattern. Astrology and horoscopes as developed by the Chinese are essentially about discerning the boundaries placed by the Way, and then describing the space for manoeuvring within those boundaries. It is the basic idea of flowing with the Way – expressed more poetically in the *Tao Te Ching* as 'Yielding you overcome; bending you are able to stand up again'(22).

It is, however, in the calendrical systems of ancient China that we can begin to see some of the earliest roots of the more philosophical dimensions of the Tao. The art of calendar-making in China is very old indeed. Certainly by the Shang dynasty (c. 1523–1028 BC), the basics of the still extant calendar system were in place. One of the oldest legends of China describes how the Emperor Yao, one of the Five August Emperors, gave orders for the construction of the calendar – as well as the reason for its construction.

> 'He commanded Hsis and Ho, in reverent accordance with (their observations of) the wide heavens, to calculate and delineate (the movements and appearances of) the sun, the moon, the stars and the divisions of the heavens, and so to deliver respectfully the seasons to be observed by the people.'
>
> (*Shu Ching*, Part 1. Book II.)

The calendar was created in order that human life could be guided and regulated by Heaven. Harmony was the basis of the calendar; it was so important that no official calendar could be issued without the approval of the Emperor. He kept an entire office of calendar-makers and astrologers solely for this purpose. Each year, as part of his role as mediator between Heaven, Earth and Humanity, the Emperor issued these calendars to all the high officials. From these calendars, the high officials then passed on to the people the rulings about times for planting and harvesting and other similar activities. The failure of the Emperor to provide such clear guidance for following the Way of Heaven and of Nature could mean the end of a dynasty. The same book in the *Shu Ching* tells us that Hsis and Ho failed to do their work properly after a few years, and chaos and disaster struck the Empire. Hsis and Ho were upbraided for having 'been the first to allow the regulations of Heaven to get into disorder'. For a calendar to give the wrong dates for harvesting or the wrong dates for an eclipse was held to be grounds for overthrowing the Emperor. If the Mandate of Heaven was not working, then it could not be Heaven's fault – it must mean that the Emperor was at fault. Throughout Chinese history, when new dynasties arose, one of the first things they did was to construct a new calendar as a sign that they were now the key players in interpreting the Way of Heaven to humanity.

As we shall see when we explore the Taoist philosophers in the next chapter, this notion of observing and following the Way of Heaven and of Nature is central to Taoism and its outlook on human behaviour. Likewise, in the text of the *Tao Te Ching* the sage/ruler reflects many of the attributes expected of the Emperor in his role as mediator and as calendar giver. At least part of the roots of the Taoist image of the sagacious ruler as the exemplar of The Way lies in the calendar-making and astrological dimensions of the role of the Emperor of ancient China, as well as in the shamanists of earliest China.

IMMORTALITY AND LONGEVITY

Finally, there is yet another strand which contributed to what eventually became Taoism. It is hard to know quite where to place this. Perhaps it was in part an influence from the shamanists – it certainly appears as one of the attributes or fields of skills of the *fang-shih*. It is the quest for immortality or for longevity. The legends of places where immortal beings dwelt who, if encountered, could tell you the secret of immortality, were certainly current around the fifth century BC and by the third century were well defined. There was the magic mountain of Kunlun in the west which, if you could reach it, would ensure you lived forever. In the opposite direction there were the magical islands in the eastern ocean, the isles of P'eng-lai, Fang-hu and Ying-chou. Ssu-ma Ch'ien tells us that as early as the middle of the fourth century BC kings were sending expeditions to try to discover these islands.

'Unfortunately, just as the men are about to reach the shores, the boats are swept back and away by the wind. In earlier times, some people actually managed to reach them: there the Blessed and the drug that prevents death can be found; there, all things, all birds and the four-footed animals are white and the palaces are made of gold and silver. . . . There is not one of the rulers who would not like to have gone there.'

There is a clue for us here. Ssu-ma Ch'ien tells us that all the rulers of ancient China wanted to go there. In other words, this quest was a part and parcel of Chinese beliefs and hopes from at least the fifth century. It belonged to no school or tradition by that time, but rather was held in common. Where it arose from, we do not know. What is certain is that by the time Taoism became a recognizable faith, the quest for immortality had become most especially linked to Taoism and even the most passing and often slighting references to the quest in the philosophical writings was taken as a coded message or formula. We will explore this in more detail later.

So what made these various streams run together, albeit not always? Why did Taoism emerge and was Taoism the only belief system or value system in China to develop the idea of the Tao – the Way? This is what the next chapter examines.

3 · LAO TZU AND FRIENDS

The Tao is older than Taoism. This is not some deeply meaningful text from a lost Taoist classic. It simply is the truth. The Tao was spoken of, studied and encountered long before Taoism as a definable philosophy or creed came into being. Nor is the term Tao exclusive to those whom we would see as being Taoists or Taoistically inclined. The Tao, as befits its true nature, is wider and older than those who claim to follow it.

It is impossible to say when the word *Tao* first began to take on the significance it now has. What we do know is that the word has evolved from very simple origins to its present multi-faceted role. Let us first look at the actual character *Tao*. In everyday Chinese vocabulary, it still has as its basic meaning, its original sense of a road, street or path. I have lived on roads such as *Tai Po Tao* which simply means the road to Tai Po. The character arises from the use of two other characters meaning 'head' and 'to go'. This combination was used to mean way or path, usually between one place and another, such as my road being the road to Tai Po.

THE TAO AS THE SPIRITUAL PATH

It is clear that while the word was originally conceived to express a path, it soon began to have wider and deeper meaning than that. The earliest recorded use of the word in a 'spiritual' or metaphorical way is in the *Shu Ching* – the Classic of History. This is a notoriously difficult document, parts of which may date from the late Shang dynasty (c.1523–1028 BC). Most of it is largely composed of materials from the Chou dynasty and Warring States (1028–221 BC). Yet it claims to contain documents from the end of the third millennium BC up to the beginning of the first millennium BC. It is therefore necessary to treat any texts from the *Shu Ching* with caution, for it is hard to know exactly when they were written. However, in the *Shu Ching* we come across the word 'Tao' in two forms in which it is to appear in the works of the Taoists, Confucians and others of the religious, social, political and philosophical world.

THE TAO AS THE PROPER WAY

In the accounts of the Shang dynasty in the *Shu Ching* we find the Tao occurring many times. In its simplest form it is just the character *Tao* and means the right and proper way that life should be conducted. So, in the *Councils of the Mighty Yu* (an Emperor who was supposed to have reigned around 2000 BC) we read the following:

> 'I see how great is your virtue, how admirable your vast achievements. The specific choice of Heaven rest upon you; you must eventually take the throne of the great ruler. The mind of humanity is restless and likely to fail; its willingness to follow the Way is small.'
>
> (*Shu Ching*, Part II: Book 2. Ch.II: 14–15.)

In the context of the story being told, it is obvious that 'Tao' here means what is the right and proper thing to do, but in more than just a plain moralistic sense. (Note also its link with virtue which is important as the *Tao Te Ching* means the Classic of The Way and Virtue.) Yu was a great hero who served his country without thought for himself. When the mighty Yellow River burst its banks, Yu fought against the waters for ten years. He travelled the country building up the river walls, canalizing the river and draining the land. So selfless was he that even when he was close to his home, he never visited it until the dreadful waters had been tamed. For later generations, he came to be one of the models of proper devotion to the doing of what was right.

In this extract from the *Shu Ching*, the Emperor is telling Yu that he will shortly become the Emperor. The Emperor reassures Yu that this is not treason but the proper Way. It is bound to come about because Yu is such an upright and honest person and thus himself embodies the Way. It is important that we note that it is in the fulfilment of duties to the state that the Way is manifest in and for Yu. This example of the political and social Way is the earliest form that we know of it and lies at the heart of Confucius' teaching.

THE TAO AS THE WAY OF HEAVEN

There is yet another use of the Tao. This is in conjunction with the character for Heaven. It is thus usually translated Heaven's Way or the Way of Heaven. In the *Shu Ching* it has a more cosmic dimension than just plain old Tao – as one might expect! It has a much stronger ethical flavour and is already linked to the kind of wisdom which we associate with the Taoist philosophers. An example is this text reputedly taken from the time of King T'ang (c1460–41 BC).

'I have heard the saying: "He who finds himself teachers, will rule the greatest area; he who says no one is his equal, will fall. He who is willing to ask, becomes greater; he who relies entirely upon himself, will be humbled and made small." So, he who wishes to be sure of his end, must look to his beginning. There is security for those who observe propriety and disaster for those who are blind and pay no attention. To revere and honour the Way of Heaven is the way to ensure the favour of Heaven for ever.'

(*Shu Ching*, Part IV. Book 2. Chapter IV. 8–9.)

Here we can begin to see the paradox or double simile so beloved of the Taoist writers. We can also begin to hear the sort of 'otherworldly', yet political advice which is so much a mark of the *Tao Te Ching*.

In these two different quotes, we can discern the beginnings of the development of the word 'Tao' from its original functional mode, to that of an abstract concept with profound layers of meaning. As I have said, it is very difficult to know how to date parts of the *Shu Ching*. We may be dealing here with elements of an oral tradition concerning these early times which has been passed down through the ages. More likely, as these texts relate to discourse rather than specific events, we are dealing with the reflections of the compiler(s). It is fairly clear that parts at least of the *Shu Ching* were edited in the seventh to eighth centuries BC. It is possible, therefore, that we are looking at texts from that period. However, as I indicated above, these texts continue to exercise the minds of Sinologists and there is remarkably little agreement about this or any other part of the *Shu Ching*.

THE I CHING

We now need to pause briefly and look at one place where the Tao is NOT mentioned, for its absence is of some significance. The oldest religious or mystical text which we have from ancient China is the *I Ching*, the Classic of Change. Its basic text – the sixty-four hexagram descriptions – dates from around the year 1000 BC; its line by line commentaries from a little later. This extraordinary book makes no mention of Tao, nor uses any such phrase. This is a significant silence. For, in the most important of the ancient commentaries – the Great Treatise – the idea of Tao is explored in great detail. Yet there is no overt mention of it in the earliest sections of the text. In part this can be explained by the very terse and cryptic nature of the basic texts. They do not go in for the sort of development of debate which is the usual context in which the Tao is specifically mentioned – as for instance in the *Chuang Tzu*. Furthermore, as I and colleagues have argued elsewhere (*The Contemporary I Ching*, Rider, 1989), the terse nature of the texts was designed exactly to allow for, or foster, the need for commentary and exposition which the Great Treatise encapsulates. Thus at one level we should not be too surprised that the word Tao is not in the *I Ching*. The entire text is in a sense concerned with what Tao came later to symbolize.

What this means is that we can probably say with some degree of certainty that the two ideas of Tao – the right pattern of behaviour and the Way of Heaven – were not in common use when the *I Ching* was being written, c.1000 BC, but began to emerge during the seventh and eighth centuries BC. In my mind there is no doubt that they were not concepts known or used by the earlier dynasties of the Hsia and Shang. The references in the *Shu Ching* are aetiological – that is to say, projections into the past of concepts of the day, the day being that of the seventh to eighth century compiler of the *Shu Ching*. This would explain why, by the time we reach the sixth to fifth centuries BC, we find a veritable explosion of thinking and reflection upon the Tao by at least two major schools – the Schools of K'ung Fu-tzu and of Lao Tzu. The term had obviously been gaining in use and popularity for some time and with the 'Age of the Philosophers' the need to define the exact use and purpose of the term had become of considerable importance. This is especially true if what we looked at in Chapter 2 is taken into account. The gradual convergence of different ideas arising from various practices – shamanism, astrology, magic, the calendar – means that as the word Tao began to be used to express something in common between all these, the need for definition became greater.

CONFUCIUS AND THE TAO

If often comes as a surprise to Westerners interested in Taoism to discover that Confucius made almost as much use of the concept Tao as did Lao Tzu. This is because in the West we see Tao as being the 'property' of Taoism – and thus as mystical. The common perception of Confucius, in contrast, makes most Westerners see him as an elevated civil servant, concerned with the mundane and institutional, and thus not the spiritual. To a great extent this is true, yet Confucius and his followers through the first four to five centuries after his death, explored and developed their own understanding of the Tao – very much along the lines of the way in which the philosophy of the Tao was enunciated in the *Shu Ching*. In popular Taoism, and in the way in which Confucius was elevated in popular belief to the status of a god – something Confucius would have found very objectionable – the two strands of meaning of Tao came back together again and merged. What we need to do, therefore, is to look at the distinctive Confucian understanding of Tao and then come, at last, to Lao Tzu and the Taoist philosophers. To jump straight to Lao Tzu ignoring Confucius would be to lose vital clues to the meaning and context of Lao Tzu's revolutionary changes to the depths of meaning of the Tao.

Confucius is the Romanised version of the proper name K'ung

Confucius

Fu-tzu, the honorific name given to the man K'ung Ch'iu, and meaning Master Teacher K'ung. Born in either 522 or 551 BC he lived, until 479 BC, during a period of great decline in China and constant feuding between rival states within the borders of historic China. A man of relatively humble origins, K'ung was an advisor to a number of the petty states which had come into existence during the decline of the Chou dynasty – a time which led to that disturbed period of Chinese history known as the Warring States (480–221 BC). K'ung seems to have tried to help hold together the old structures in order to avoid precisely the sort of anarchy and warfare which actually ensued. In trying to impose order and retain structures, he looked affectionately back to a golden age of Chinese life, government and social relationships. To K'ung, correct government was a matter of both internal and external correctness. The empire or state should be ruled by a master who combined the pragmatic skills of a ruler with the sagacity of a wise man. Such a personality would express itself in terms of a well run government, one in which things were done according to the correct way. Part of this correct way would be manifest in abiding by the proper rules for behaviour, relationships and ritual. It is this ritual/rules aspect of K'ung which now strikes us as very fussy and old-fashioned. Take for instance this account of K'ung's rather abrupt departure from the state of Lu, where he was the head of Justice. Mencius (*Meng Tzu* – *Master Meng*; fourth century BC) records the following:

> 'When K'ung Tzu was chief minister of Justice in Lu, the prince started to ignore his advice. Soon after there were the sacrifices for the solstice. When K'ung Tzu was not offered a piece of the sacrificial meat, he left without even stopping to take off his ceremonial hat. Those who did not know him, assumed he had taken offence because of the meat. Those who knew him, realized that is was because the proper rituals had not been observed.'
>
> (*Meng Tzu*, Book VI. Part II. Chapter VI.)

K'ung was convinced that if the outward signs of correct behaviour could be instilled in a state, then this would curb the worse aspects of kingly individualism and personal corruption. To this end he travelled much of his life trying to teach or guide leaders into proper behaviour, ritual and observances, hoping thus to reform or reshape the inner man. He failed, but the period of the Warring States brought greater and greater appeal to his teachings, so that they seemed to offer a very attractive alternative to the anarchy and selfishness of that period. He was a man whose interests lay in the realm of the political and social state and thus he came to be seen as the antithesis of the traditional 'Taoist' approach to life, though as we shall see, Lao Tzu was at times closer to K'ung's ideal of service than to the later 'Taoist' ideal of withdrawal. There are some very unflattering things said about K'ung by the Taoists, yet K'ung sought in his own life to follow the Way. At times, his understanding of the idea of Tao is very close to that of Lao Tzu. What is interesting is that both writers were concerned in their writings with the right and proper way to run a state. Both saw the Tao as being important to this process. Where they differ is that K'ung sought to wed the Tao to a rigid set of values and virtues which would of themselves create the gentlemen who would rule wisely. It is with this idea that we shall start to look at K'ung's use of the term Tao.

At one level K'ung uses Tao to express a rather staid concept of moral righteousness and correct behaviour. For example, in Book 4:5 of *The Analects*:

31

'The Master said: Riches and honours are what people want. If these cannot be gained in the proper way (tao), they should not be kept. Poverty and meanness are what people dislike. If it had been obtained in the right way (tao) then I would not try to avoid them.'

The sense here is very clearly that the way being described is the proper or recognised way of moral behaviour. Thus, if a person has behaved properly in trade and has made money and received honours, then that is fine. It could not be further from the usual Taoist stance that to become involved with such a pursuit is in itself a deviation from the Way. In a later book of The Analects, Book 16:2, K'ung begins to use the Tao in a somewhat broader sense – not dissimilar to texts in the Tao Te Ching:

'K'ung Tzu said: When the Way prevails in the world, the rites, music and punitive military expeditions are initiated by the Emperor (Son of Heaven). When the Way does not prevail in the world, they are initiated by the lesser lords. . . . When the Way prevails in the world, policy is not in the hands of the Counsellors. When the Way prevails in the world, there is nothing for the ordinary people to argue about.'

This text is very similar to texts like the Tao Te Ching, Chapters 17 and 18:

'When his (the sage's) work is done, the people say "It happened to us naturally."'

'When the state falls into darkness and is troubled, then loyal ministers appear.'

Finally, K'ung uses the Tao in a sense which is virtually identical with the way it is used by Lao Tzu. An example ascribed to him and appearing in the first few lines of the opening of The Doctrine of the Mean runs as follows:

'What Heaven has given is called the law of Nature. To follow this natural way is to follow the Way. To nurture this Way is called learning. The Way must not be left, even for a moment. If it could be left, then it would not be the Way.'

At times K'ung seems to be very close to the Taoist attitude, as when he says, 'He has not died in vain, who dies on the day he learns about the Way.' (Book 4:8 of *The Analects*.) But when it comes down to it, what K'ung is really interested in is correct behaviour. This emerges when he lays out his total schema in synopsis as he does in the following quote: 'I set my mind on the Way, base myself on virtue, lean upon benevolence for support and seek relaxation in the cultured arts.'

The other term which figures large in both the *Tao Te Ching* and K'ung's teachings, is the Te. The *Tao Te Ching* is after all the Classic of the Tao and the Te – the Classic of The Way and of Virtue. For K'ung the Te was of equal importance to the Tao. For K'ung, virtue was the personal manifestation of following the Way. Indeed, without it there was little point in trying. According to K'ung, virtue comes from Heaven. 'Heaven is the source of the virtue (te) which I have.' In essence, K'ung's use of the term Te in his writings is remarkably similar to the way Lao Tzu develops it in the second half of the *Tao Te Ching*. However, in later Confucian thinking, the practice of virtue (Te) was to become of greater importance than the Way. Indeed, one could almost argue that, for many Confucians, Te became the Tao!

In terms of the areas of real difference and development between K'ung's thinking and that of Lao Tzu, it is the Tao which is of prime interest. Putting it crudely, K'ung ultimately sees the Way as being a rule which Heaven has given and which binds all under Heaven (the world) to follow it. This rule is hierarchical and ends in the definitions of filial relationships with their clear and unbending ranking and status. Furthermore, K'ung sees rewards in the material world as being a sign of the success of following the Way. All this goes against what emerged as Taoist philosophy, and this divergence of the Way is very clearly captured in the stories of the meeting of K'ung and Lao Tzu. So now it is time for us to look at Lao Tzu and at what he did with this broadly defined, powerful concept of the Way.

LAO TZU

Did Lao Tzu ever exist? Again, what sounds like a sentence out of the first half of the *Tao Te Ching* is, in fact, a valid question which vexed even the earliest historical writers of China. The earliest 'biography' of Lao Tzu was compiled by Ssu-ma Ch'ien (first century BC). Or rather, he tried to write such a biography! In introducing the details he has gleaned, he tells the reader that he found it very difficult and that he is mystified at the lack of specific information. All that he can really say is that Lao Tzu was born at the village of Chu Jen in the area of Lai, the county of Hu in the state of Ch'u. His surname was Li, his personal name was Erh and his public name was Tan. Chu Jen has become the town of Luyi and visitors can still see the temple raised over the reputed place of birth of Lao Tzu. However, as we shall see, we may need to treat the shrines of Luyi with some caution.

One thing we have to realize is that the name 'Lao Tzu' is not Lao Tzu's name. It is simply an honorific title meaning Old Master. His real name, according to Ssu-ma Ch'ien was Li Erh Tan. Yet there are scholars who fear that even this may be untrue. At the end of Ssu-ma Ch'ien's biography he gives a genealogy which claims to show that the then extant Li family from Shantung were the direct descendents of Lao Tzu. Some writers such as Kaltenmark (*Lao Tzu and Taoism*) think that the Li family wanted to claim him as an illustrious ancestor and that the surname Li was given by them to Lao Tzu. I must say that I feel this is being too fastidious. I see no valid reason to doubt that the Li family claimed such a descent because Lao Tzu's real surname was Li. However, this issue goes to show just how uncertain scholarship is about every aspect of the historical Lao Tzu.

Ssu-ma Ch'ien goes on to tell us that Lao Tzu was the court archivist of the Chou state. This is a relatively minor post. Of greater importance is the assertion that K'ung visited and talked with Lao Tzu. There are two extant accounts within Ssu-ma Ch'ien's history of what was said at this meeting plus many rather scurrilous accounts in later Taoist literature and some not so friendly accounts in later Confucian books regarding further meetings! It is worth reading both accounts for they give some flavour of the philosophical differences and differences of outlook between the two men. Whether the meeting ever actually took place, where, when and so forth, we cannot say. There is a wide range of descriptions given in later books. What was said and who came off best depends on whether you read the Confucian books or the Taoists! As for what the Buddhists say happened, that is another story and not flattering to either Confucius or Lao Tzu. So let us simply read Ssu-ma Ch'ien's account.

'When K'ung visited Chou he asked Lao Tzu to tutor him in the rites. Lao Tzu replied, "The very bones of those you talk about have turned to dust. All that remains of them is their words. You know that when a noble lives in times which are good, he travels to court in a carriage. But when times are difficult, he goes where the wind blows. Some say that a wise merchant hides his wealth and thus seems poor. Likewise the sage, if he has great internal virtue, seems on the outside to be a fool. Stop being so arrogant; all those demands; that self-importance and your over-keen enthusiasm. None of this is true to yourself. That is all I have to say to you." K'ung left and said to his followers, "I know that a bird can fly; that fishes swim; that animals can run. Things that run can be trapped in nets. What can swim can be caught in traps. Those that fly can be shot down with arrows. But what to do with the dragon I do not know. It rises on the clouds and the wind. Today I have met Lao Tzu and he is like a dragon."'

The second accounts goes as follows:

'When K'ung was leaving Lao Tzu said to him, "I have heard people say that someone who is wealthy and in authority gives his guests gifts of money and that a sage gives gifts of words. I am not a man of either wealth or authority; maybe I am sometimes a sage. So I will give you words as your gift. The man who is wise and clear-sighted will soon die because his criticisms of other people are appropriate. Such a man with such insight puts his life on the line because he shows up other people's weaknesses and faults. The man who knows himself to be a son no longer belongs just to himself. Also the man who knows himself to be a subject no longer belongs to himself."'

So we have a name, Li, a birthplace, Luyi and a meeting with K'ung – all of which raise problems, but let us press on. What else do we know about Lao Tzu? The answer is very little. The only other thing

35

that Ssu-ma Ch'ien could report was the final journey of Lao Tzu. Despairing of the world of the small Chinese states, Lao Tzu left Chou and set off for the West. Reaching the pass in the mountains at Han-ku, he stopped for the night with the keeper of the gate. The keeper, Kuan Yin, realizing what a sage he had staying with him, and knowing that he would never be seen again, begged Lao Tzu to write down his thoughts. Lao Tzu did, and the resulting book was the *Tao Te Ching*. Having written this, Lao Tzu passed through the gate and was never seen again.

This is a wonderful story, but is not what it seems at first. First of all, the term 'going West' means to die. In Chinese mythology, the West was the land of wonders and of the afterlife. It was the mysterious magical world. It was where the just and noble went to live after their death. This tradition continues to this day in that Japanese Buddhism talks about the Land in the West as the place of the future Heaven. Secondly Kuan Yin is not just an ordinary doorkeeper with a literary or publishing bent. He is, in fact, worshipped as a deity himself. So the request for the teachings was a request from the gods for the wisdom of Lao Tzu to be written down before he died. Thirdly, whatever else the *Tao Te Ching* is, it is not a book written by one man in one night!

Lao Tzu departing for the West

What are we to make of this exit? Certainly, the language used would have conveyed to contemporaries that Lao Tzu was talking about death. Equally certainly, later Taoists took it to mean Lao Tzu did literally travel West and never returned. In anti-Buddhist books of the fourth to ninth centuries, Taoist writers would claim that Lao Tzu travelled West until he came to North India where he taught the Buddha. Sadly, the Taoist writers say, the Buddha didn't really grasp Lao Tzu's finer points! Yet fellow Taoists of the same period were also busy building fine monuments at Lao Tzu's home town of Luyi. These monuments are supposed to cover the graves of Lao Tzu and his mother. So what are we to make of all this?

It seems likely that someone lived around the fifth century BC who was known as the Old Master. Who he was, what he did and what he taught we shall probably never know. In the end all those questions are unanswerable and, as far as the development of Taoism is concerned, ultimately unimportant. At some time over the next hundred years or so, sayings were ascribed to this Old Master until a veritable collection had been gathered. These were then written down as the words of Lao Tzu himself.

I think it is important to realize how elusive Lao Tzu is before we proceed to look at 'his' words. The reason is very simple. Whoever Lao Tzu was, he was not a Taoist. Whatever he said, he did not say it as a Taoist. Those who collected his thoughts and edited what we know as Lao Tzu's *Tao Te Ching* did not see themselves as Taoists. Indeed, the title *Tao Te Ching*, with its emphasis on the 'Tao', was not the original title given to the book. It was originally called the *Lao Tzu*. It was only in the early Han period (second century BC) that the term Taoist was invented. Before that time there were, as we noted earlier, scores of different 'Schools', each with their different teachings and Masters. Around these figures clustered a steadily developing corpus of materials and ideas, much of which was written long after the original founder figure was dead. Yet the practice then, as with so many other cultures, was to ascribe any significant writing to the original Master. This was not deceit. It was the highest form of honour that you could give to your original Master and inspirer.

We need to avoid looking at this from the perspective of the twentieth century. Nowadays, we have a very strong sense of proprietorial rights over the use of names. If, for instance, I was a great admirer of Martin Luther King and wanted to write about the justice of the struggle of black people today, it would never dawn on me to write the book and then claim Martin Luther King had written it! I would be taken to court immediately, or to the asylum for having thought a man who was dead could write a book about today! However, in ancient cultures, this is exactly what did happen. In the Bible, we have the tradition that Moses wrote the Five Books of the Torah – the Pentateuch. Yet these self-same books record the death of Moses and events after his death! So it is with Lao Tzu. What we have in the *Tao Te Ching* and in the other book ascribed to the pen of Lao Tzu, the *T'ai Shang Kan Ying P'ien*, are thoughts and teachings collected over a period of maybe a century or more and ascribed to the founder figure Lao Tzu, while in the *T'ai Shang Kan Ying P'ien* we have thoughts and stories collected over possibly five to six hundred years, yet still ascribed to Lao Tzu.

Yet Lao Tzu, whoever he was, was not a Taoist. This is the other significant point which needs to be made. Lao Tzu's teachings, and the collection of teachings which became associated with his name, led to the foundation of a group who called themselves Taoists. As far as Lao Tzu was concerned, he was as much a Teist as a Taoist – as the title of the *Tao Te Ching* says! Or to put it a little less dramatically, Lao Tzu was exploring similar issues to those explored by K'ung, but developed his thinking in a very different direction to that of K'ung – a direction which later generations called Taoism, but to which Lao Tzu and his followers seem to have never given a name.

As we shall see in later chapters, Lao Tzu's role in Taoism changes dramatically and the legends which arise about him leave any historical persona far behind. The role of key figures in any faith is almost always thus. They are as important for what later generations ascribed to them as for what they actually were, for it is their role as figures of faith rather than of history which has helped to shape the religion. In lacking any real evidence of the existence of Lao Tzu, we need not feel that Taoism has a hole at its centre. Whether Lao Tzu ever existed, did the things he is supposed to have done, wrote the words ascribed to him is, ultimately in terms of the faith, irrelevant. For it is what people believed he was, did and wrote which has shaped history for nearly twenty-five centuries.

Let us therefore look at this extraordinary book, the *Tao Te Ching*.

THE TAO TE CHING

The title *Tao Te Ching* is capable of a number of translations. The word 'ching' simply means a classic. This title was only given to the book in the Han period, somewhere between the first century BC and the first century AD. Even then, it was using the word rather loosely. The *Tao Te Ching* was, in fact, only ever counted as one of the formal classics of China during the T'ang dynasty. The family name of the T'ang emperors was Li, the same as Lao Tzu's. They considered themselves to be descendants of his and thus raised the *Tao Te Ching* to the status of a formal classic.

The two other words were added at the same time as the Ching, namely during the Han dynasty. They reflect the traditional division of the text into two sections. The first section, Chapters 1 to 37, opens with the definition of Tao and then explores it in detail. The second section, Chapters 38 to 81, opens with the definition of Te and then continues to discuss the Tao, with various references or further chapters on Te. Hence the title the Classic of Tao and Te. Before this title was accorded to the text, it was simply known as the *Lao Tzu*. This is in line with the reasons we looked at above regarding why the text is ascribed to Lao Tzu. It also follows the traditional pattern of titling books after the Master. Hence we have the *Meng Tzu* (Mencius) the *Chuang Tzu* and the *Lieh Tzu*, all named after their original teacher figures. It is significant that as the *Lao Tzu* grew in importance under the Han dynasty, it was retitled in order to stress its special importance and to set it above the others such as the *Chuang Tzu* and the *Lieh Tzu*.

It is perhaps worth noting that the earliest extant text which we have has the two sections the other way round. This text, found in funeral goods in a tomb dated 168 BC, has section two first. Thus the book becomes the *Te Tao Ching*, though there is no actual title to the book found in the grave. The pre-Han writer Han-fei Tzu also put the sections round the other way when he wrote about the *Lao Tzu*, so it is interesting to note that for some time at least, the Te could be legitimately seen as the foremost part of the book.

The problem with *Tao Te* is how best to translate it. Arthur Waley calls it 'the Way and its power'. Needham has 'Canon of the Virtue of the Tao'. The word Te is the problem. It is open to a number of interpretations, but with two main ones emerging as leading contenders: 'Virtue' and 'Power/authority'. It is assumed by most translators that the word Te is in a subservient role to Tao in the title, as indeed it is in the actual text. Hence, whatever role Te has it is in support of Tao, as indicated in the translations of Waley and Needham. So take your pick, for there is no right answer! From now on I shall simply refer to it as the *Tao Te Ching*.

As a book, it falls into a category of ancient literature along side other such classics as the *I Ching* and *Ch'un Ch'iu*. Each of these books uses short, pithy statements which are obviously meant to stand on their own – that is, there is usually no clear link with what comes next. They are also designed to require a commentary either orally, by a diviner or scholar, or in writing.

The *I Ching* is a very good example. Written initially sometime around the year 1000 BC, it is China's oldest extant book. Its distinctive style is that of short sentences which give the minimum of information and leave the reader to use his or her own understanding to fit it into a specific context. Even when the reader is able to do this, it still requires a professional *I Ching* reader or commentary to help reveal the many possible layers of meaning within the text. Thus for example, hexagram 41 has this text to introduce it:

> 'Injured. Have confidence. Supreme good fortune and no regrets. Proper behaviour is possible. It is good to advance when fully prepared. Two baskets of offerings may be better than offerings which are expensive.'

Not immediately comprehensible, except in a very simplistic way, by the average reader! Furthermore, the hexagrams on either side, 40 and 42, do not seem to have any link with number 41. Hexagram 40 says:

> 'Let loose. There are advantages in the southwest. If there is nothing else to be done there is good fortune in his returning. If he has to go anywhere it will be more fortunate to travel early.'

40

while hexagram 42 says:

> 'Increase. It is helpful to go forward with plans in mind. It is good to cross the great river.'

It is as if each hexagram stands entirely on its own, like a collection of proverbs with nothing to link them except the fact that they are proverbs. Added to this is the obscurity of the meaning, necessitating, as I have said above, commentary.

The Ch'un Ch'iu is similar in many ways to this. The title means Spring and Autumn Annals. It is a chronicle of the events of each year in and around the State of Lu from 722 BC to 481 BC. Its significance to the Chinese is that it is one of the Confucian Five Classics – along with the I Ching, the Shu Ching (Book of History), the Shih Ching (Book of Poems) and the Li Chi (Book of Rites). K'ung is supposed to have written the Ch'un Ch'iu and its bare, sparse lines have been scoured by Confucian scholars ever since for the deeper meaning that they are supposed to contain. Now, whilst this text does have a chronological link between one chapter and another, it still manifests the same basic pattern as the I Ching, that is to say, pithy text; no link between one statement and another, other than that they are bunched under a certain year; and the need for commentary to make any sense of them. An example is this from Book VI, Year 18 of Duke Wan (608 BC).

> 'In the spring of his eighteenth year, in the second month of the King on Ting-ch'ou day, the duke died beneath his towers.
>
> Ying, earl of Ts'in died.
>
> In the summer, during the fifth month, on the day of Wu Hsu the people of Ts'e murdered their ruler, Shang Yin.
>
> In the sixth month, on the day of Kuei Yu, we buried our ruler, duke Wan.
>
> In the autumn, the duke's son Sui and Shu-sun Ti-shin went to Ts'e.
>
> In the winter during the tenth month, the son died.
>
> The wife, lady Kung returned to Ts'e.
>
> Ki-sun Hang Fou went to Ts'e.

41

Kiu murdered its ruler Shu-Ki.'

From these simple pieces of information, you would be amazed at
what Confucian scholars tell us it all really means!

The point I am making is that the terse, non-sequential nature
of the *Tao Te Ching* is typical of both the limits (or alternatively
the possibilities) inherent in the very basic nature of much ancient
Chinese writing style, and is typical in requiring explanation and
commentary. It seems highly likely that texts such as the *Tao Te
Ching*, the *I Ching* and the *Ch'un Ch'iu* arose from pieces of oral
wisdom which were collected and then strung together rather like
pearls on a cord. Each is distinct, rounded and polished by time
and telling, yet together they give a sense of unity of purpose. These
collections of sayings would always have been quoted, recalled and
passed on in the context of discussion, debate and commentary. Our
difficulty today, whether we are Chinese approaching our ancient
texts or Westerners discovering these fascinating documents for
the first time, is that we have largely lost the context in which
the texts were given; we do not think like the ancients and many
of the characters have actually changed their meaning so totally
over the centuries as to present real problems of interpretation.
We are also confronted at times with symbols and images, the
true meaning of which have been lost and at which we can only
hazard a guess. Perhaps, however, it is precisely this difficulty and
vagueness about these texts which so attracts us, for what we are
compelled to do is to try to make sense of the texts within our own
context, while modifying this by trying to understand as much as
possible about the intellectual and actual context from which they
originally emerged.

Having now looked at the literary context of the *Tao Te Ching*,
we need to note that the *Tao Te Ching* marks a development. While
the text is still very terse and while the chapters only occasionally
have any direct discernible link to those before and after them,
the *Tao Te Ching*'s isolated pearls of wisdom, strung together,
do exhibit a far deeper exploration of each theme than others
of that genre. Each chapter of the *Tao* is in itself a mixture of
the one-liner with some exposition. As such, it offers the reader
more of an inherent understanding within the actual text than
either the *I Ching* or the *Ch'un Ch'iu*. Take for instance Chapter
25:

'Some thing is mysteriously brought into existence,
long before Heaven or Earth is made.
It is silent and shapeless,
It has no equal.
It is always present, endlessly in motion.
From it, like from a mother, everything living has come.
I do not know what to call it.
So I shall call it Tao.
Reluctantly I shall call it the Greatest.

Being the greatest, it goes everywhere.
Silently it fills all.

So I say the Tao is greatest.
It is greater than Heaven itself.
Heaven is greater than Earth.
The Earth is greater than the ruler.
These are the four greatest and the ruler is one of them.

Humans learn from the Earth.
The Earth follows Heaven.
Heaven is led by the Tao.
The Tao is simply the natural way.'

While this text is full of profound meaning which requires study and reflection, it is also a commentary on itself, developing an idea and image and reiterating this. As such, the *Tao Te Ching* offers far more than either the *I Ching* or the *Ch'un Ch'iu* – which is presumably why it has always been so popular. Chapter 39 is another good example of a saying, amplification of the saying and commentary:

'All things from the beginning of time came from the One.
The sky is clear and quiet.
The earth is peaceful and supportive.
The deity is good and powerful.
The valley is able to carry all.
All things are well and living.
The king is blessed and the country is well ruled by him.
All these virtues come from being in harmony.

If the sky were not clear, it would fall.
If the earth were not supportive, it would crumble.

43

If the deity were not good, it would be despised.
If the valley were not empty, it could not hold things.
If all things were not fed by virtue, they would die.
If the kings were not just, they would have revolts on their hands.

Remember, without the humble there can be no mighty.
Without the foundations there can be no higher place.
Kings call themselves the lonely ones. By this humility they are
actually the highest.
To be too successful is to be on the path to defeat.
To be a jade is very rare and thus important,
Whereas to be like everyone else is to be like sand – common.'

THE PHILOSOPHY OF THE TAO TE CHING

So what is the *Tao Te Ching*'s essential message? I think it is an
impossible question to answer precisely because the *Tao Te Ching*
was not written by one person following a logical sequence of
argument. Nor did the compiler try to give it more than a basic
shape, such as the Tao section and the Te section. Nor are we
dealing with a book which consciously set out to present the
'Taoists' case – for, as we noted earlier, Taoism and Taoists did
not exist as distinct self-conscious communities when the book was
created. Again, we may be looking at precisely one of the reasons
why the book is so popular. Because it does not have one central
idea which it systematically develops, it is a far more interesting
and challenging text than, say, K'ung's writings with their logical
development of ideas.

We therefore need to approach the book aware of the fact that
wherever we open it, we shall be able to encounter a nugget of
wisdom, teaching, commentary and imagery which by itself will
set us thinking. This is indeed exactly how books such as the *Tao
Te Ching* or the *I Ching* have been used in personal devotions down
the centuries in China.

What we can of course say is that the text explores the issues of
knowledge, of time, of language and meaning, of the Way and of the
material and the non-material. It seeks to shatter the complacency of
our conventional use of language by showing its severe limitations.
It seeks to render helpless our desire to quantify and control reality.
This it does by certain key ideas or arguments which crop up

throughout the text. Take language as an example. The book opens with a discussion of the inability of language to express, or even come close to, reality.

'The Tao that is spoken of is not the eternal nature of the Tao. That which can be named is not the true Tao.'

(*Tao Te Ching*, Chapter 1.)

Along with this indefinability is its fundamental power and authority. It simply is the foundation, the roots, the source of everything, as the text earlier from Chapter 25 stresses. The Tao, in the thinking of the *Tao Te Ching*, has moved from being a foundational block of reality to being not just reality itself, but the unformed origin of all that is and of all that is yet to be. Chapter 32 illustrates both the inability of language to grasp the Tao, the inability of that which the Tao creates to control Tao, and the rootedness of all life within the Tao.

'The Tao is ultimately and forever indefinable.
Insignificant as it may be in its shapeless form, it is impossible to grasp it.
If the mighty rulers could capture it,
all life would obey them.
Heaven and Earth could be drawn together
and soothing rain made to fall.
The people would never again need to be taught
and all things would live as they should.'

THE TAO TE CHING AS A MANUAL OF KINGSHIP

Alongside this profound philosophy of language, meaning and origins lies a second major strand which crops up time and time again within the text. This is the sense of the book being a sort of manual of kingship. At frequent intervals throughout the text, pragmatic and sagacious advice is offered on how to rule the people. This can vary from the moral exhortation of not showing off in front of your subjects to how to rule in such a way as to be flowing with the Way, in order that the people are unaware you are ruling them. It is not accidental that many versions of the Tao have appeared recently in the West, which purport to be a leadership handbook for everything from world government to corporate management.

45

The *Tao Te Ching* contains a great deal of practical advice coupled with ideas designed to make rulers stop and think. An example which combines the two is the issue of warfare. Chapters 30 and 31 touch on this.

> 'Where troops have been camped
> only wild useless plants will grow.
> When an army marches through,
> the harvest will be ruined.'

> 'If you use force, you will face becoming weak.
> This is not the Way of Tao.'

> 'When people die because of a war,
> the ruler should mourn for their deaths.
> Any victory should be treated like a funeral.'

The advice above is obviously highly relevant to any ruler or his mighty nobles. But the *Tao Te Ching* also has wisdom of a very simple yet important nature to impart to any in positions of authority as in Chapter 44.

> 'Which is more important?
> Your fame or your true self?
> Your true self or your wealth,
> which is ultimately the more valuable

It comes as something of a surprise to many that the Taoists should have as their most important book a text which seems at one level to condone power, authority and domination as being valid ways for Taoist wisdom to be used. One thinks of the anti-authority stances of the later Taoist sages; of the utter renunciation of such means by the sages living alone in the mountains; of the disdain with which the immortals view such pursuits. Yet here in the *Tao Te Ching* we find not only an acceptance of such means but instructions on being effective within them. Why?

The answer lies in the two points made earlier on. This text is no one writer's view but a collection of wisdom sayings with commentary. Secondly, the Taoism of the sages and philosophers of the Han dynasty onwards did not exist when this text was being created. In the traditional telling of the life story of Lao Tzu, Taoists stress two things. Like K'ung, he was a minor official for most of his life, serving a nation state faithfully. Then, when he left the state it was out of disgust for the bad management of the state – just the same reason as K'ung gives – not because he rejected the right of the state to exist per se.

THE USE OF PARADOX

The other great element in the *Tao Te Ching* is its use of paradox. Paradox is used to force us to rethink, or even on occasions to show us that our attempts to think and to rationalize are doomed to failure. It is a very distinctive feature of the text and one which is echoed in later Taoist writings such as the *Chuang Tzu* and the *Lieh Tzu*.

> 'In this way the sage knows without exploring;
> He sees without having looked;
> He achieves without doing.'
>
> (*Tao Te Ching*, Chapter 47.)

> 'Give way and overcome.
> Bend and become straight.
> Empty yourself and be full.
> Use up things and they are new.'
>
> (*Tao Te Ching*, Chapter 22.)

Lao Tzu explains why paradox or opposites are so important in understanding the Way.

> 'Mercifulness is recognized by people because they know the opposite which is meanness.
>
> The people only know about good because there is also evil.
>
> Difficult and easy are to be found in all tasks.
> Long and short exist because you can compare them.
> High and low exist because of each other.'
>
> (*Lao Tzu*, Chapter 2.)

In the *Tao Te Ching*, the assumption is that any reality which can be glimpsed must be paradoxical or, at the very least, a balancing act between opposites. In this, the text follows the

47

traditional Chinese understanding that reality is composed of two opposite forces known as yin and yang. These forces are simply natural forces, not gods or divine powers with a mind of their own. They represent the great opposites, with yin being the female, the cold, the soft, the wet and so forth, while the yang is the male, the hot, the hard and the dry and so on. In Chinese thought, life is kept spinning by the constant struggle between these two opposite forces of yin and yang to dominate each other. Yet at precisely the point when one seems to have the upper hand, that is when it begins to decline. Thus when the weather is most yin, deep winter, that is the point at which Nature begins to move towards spring and summer, yang.

It seems that these ideas of yin and yang were first beginning to take specific shape around the time of the *Tao Te Ching's* compilation in the fifth to third centuries BC. Lao Tzu includes them in what many have seen as the fundamental creedal statement of the cosmic nature of Tao.

> 'The Tao is the origin of the One.
> The One created the two.
> The two formed the three.
> From the three came forth all life.
>
> All things are caught up with yin and carry yang within.
> When they combine, then the energy (ch'i) of life is created.'
>
> (*Tao Te Ching*, Chapter 42.)

The Tao is given as being the origin beyond the original. From Tao comes origin. From this origin come the two forces of yin and yang. From them comes the triad of Heaven, Earth and Humanity. From these come all forms of existence. This, in brief, is the synopsis of existence given by the *Tao Te Ching*. As such, we can see how far it has evolved from the very limited meaning of the word Tao, or even the concept of the Heavenly Tao which had developed in the centuries before the fifth century BC. We can also appreciate that it goes far beyond the rather formal and functional understanding which K'ung had of Tao.

NON-ACTION

No survey of the *Tao Te Ching* is complete without looking at Lao Tzu's most difficult idea, the idea of non-action. The Chinese phrase is *wu-wei* and it really is hard to find an adequate term in English. The usual translation is that of 'non-action'. Yet this is ironically too passive, for the idea of *wu-wei* is that you achieve things because you do nothing, but travel with the force or Way of Tao. Sometime it is interpreted as being total inactivity – and as such it was interpreted by the Seven Sages of the Bamboo Grove, an extraordinary bunch of drunken poets of the third century AD, of whom more in a later chapter. *Wu-wei* is the art of being. It is the art of being in such harmony with the Tao that everything happens as it should – not forced, not sought after, not planned, not bought, not desired – it just happens. Here lies the seed which was to turn the later Taoists away from roles in state government and away from the ambitions of power and authority.

With these developments, the seed was sown for the development which we know as the School of Tao – the *Tao Chia*. It is to the two other great works of philosophical Taoism that we now need to turn – and to discover that there is one thing missing from the *Tao Te Ching* which is a hallmark of these later books. And that is a wonderful and at times wicked sense of humour!

THE CHUANG TZU

Can we really call this a 'Taoist' text? I'm not sure. As we saw earlier, 'Taoism' as a classification only came to be applied to writings like those of Lao Tzu, Chuang Tzu and Lieh Tzu long after their deaths, and even long after the compilations which bear their names were rounded off. They did not call themselves Taoist. They were simply exploring issues which were pertinent to their age and culture. That later on they were bunched together is our problem, not theirs! We need to bear this in mind when reading or approaching Chuang Tzu, for we must not force him into a role which he never saw himself as having. After all, his is a book which mentions and tells nearly twice as many stories about K'ung (Confucius) as it does about Lao Tzu. This is a book which, while it makes use of some common ideas from the *Tao Te Ching*, never states that it is quoting from the *Tao Te Ching*, and only on a couple of occasions does it use texts almost certainly from the *Tao Te Ching*, while it does cite the *Annals of Spring and Autumn* by K'ung. This is a book so different from the cryptic, minimalist language of the *Tao Te Ching*, as to belong almost to another planet!

The book certainly does explore the concept of Tao. It also explores many other ideas drawn from the philosophical schools of its time. It does deal with those seeking immortality, but at times it is hard to know whether Chuang Tzu is praising or mocking them. It continues the *Tao Te Ching*'s idea that language cannot define, but in doing so, also breaks the boundaries set by language. While it has some sombre moments of reflection (not unlike the *Tao Te Ching*) the bulk of it is anecdote, jokes, practical tricks, stories and the such like – in fact one of the most enjoyable books in Chinese! So what is 'Taoist' about it? This we will have to find out as we explore this most interesting of books, which sadly has never achieved the fame in the West it deserves.

CHUANG TZU – THE MAN

Needless to say, the *Chuang Tzu* being a 'Taoist' book, we know virtually nothing at all about its supposed author. Chuang Tzu lived during the reign of King Hui of Liang (c.370–320 BC) and that of King Hsuan of Ch'i (319–301 BC) during the Warring States era. He was born in the county of Meng in the Kingdom of Sung, present day Honan. His family name was Chuang and his given name was Chou. It seems he was also called Tzu-hsiu. Ssu-ma Ch'ien has very little extra to tell except that Chuang Tzu leant towards the ideas of Lao Tzu but was interested in all the schools of his day. Ssu-ma Ch'ien, the early Han historian, records what an excellent writer he was and how lively his wit was. He relates one story about Chuang Tzu which captures something of this fascinating man.

'King Wen of Ch'u had heard of Chuang Tzu's skills and sent a messenger to him with hordes of valuable gifts. He invited him to come and be a minister in his court. Chuang Tzu laughing, told the Ch'u messenger: "A thousand pounds of gold is a fine present. To be offered a ministry is a great honour. But have you looked on the ox being taken to the sacrifice? It is fattened up for a number of years and then dressed in wonderful cloth and brought to the main shrine. At that point it probably would much prefer to be an ordinary little pig, but unfortunately it is too late. Get lost! Do not insult me. I would much rather play in the mud than be in hock to the King. I shall never become a minister, because I shall always be free to live as I want."'

Unlike Lao Tzu, we can be fairly certain that Chuang Tzu either wrote much of the book which bears his name, or his disciples collected many genuine stories about him. However, like all other great figures at that time, he also attracted other stories which were probably originally nothing to do with him. As we saw with Lao Tzu, this was not fraud or deception by the compilers, but a way of honouring a great man. There is considerable debate as to which of the thirty-three chapters of the extant text of the *Chuang Tzu* were originally anything to do with Chuang Tzu. However, it is usually agreed that the so-called Inner Chapters represent the writing of a mind which is more consistent and superior than that of those who composed the remaining chapters. The Inner Chapters are the first seven. It is almost certain that amongst the remaining twenty-five there are substantial chunks from the same pen or mind, but the text has been much butchered over the centuries. The edition now taken as standard is that of Kuo Hsiang (fourth century AD) with thirty-three chapters. However, we know that Ssu-ma Piao edited a fifty-two chapter version at the same time, while a little earlier in the third century AD Hsiang Hsiu had a twenty-seven chapter version. Such differences must make us view the extant text with a little caution!

Despite the fact that we need to be careful in approaching the text, what is evident from the seven chapters at least is that we are in the company of a man whose vitality, sense of humour and fun and liveliness of mind makes him as appealing today as he obviously was so many centuries ago. Unlike the *Tao Te Ching* in which no personality comes across, the *Chuang Tzu* positively reeks of it.

The style of the *Chuang Tzu* is story-telling and argument. And for Chuang Tzu there was no greater friend than the one who totally disagreed with what he said! In particular there was one friend whose views Chuang Tzu loved to confound. This is Hui Shih sometimes called Hui Tzu. Let us look at a sample of the sort of debates which they enjoyed.

'Chuang Tzu and Hui Tzu were walking beside the weir on the river Hao when Chuang Tzu said: "Do you see how the fish are coming to the surface and swimming around as they please.

That's what fish really enjoy." Hui Tzu replied: "You're not a fish, how can you say you know what fish enjoy?"

Chuang Tzu said: "You are not me, so how can you know I don't know what it is fish enjoy?"

Hui Tzu said: "I am not you, so I certainly don't know what it is you know. However, you are certainly not a fish and that proves that you don't know what fish really enjoy."

Chuang Tzu said: "Ah, but let's return to the original question you raised if you don't mind. You asked me how I could know what it is that fish really enjoy. Therefore you already knew I knew it when you asked the question. And I know it by being here on the edge of the river Hao.'"

(*Chuang Tzu*, Chapter 17.)

Chuang Tzu could be very rude about Hui Tzu – which I suspect was returned by Hui Tzu in the nature of a true friendship! For instance in Chapter 33 we have a survey of the different philosophical schools of the time. Here we find Hui Tzu's teachings parodied. Essentially, Hui Tzu was developing ideas related to the Tao which went towards the school of Mo Tzu who believed that all people were both worthy of and capable of love because they all came from the one source. Hui Tzu went even further and claimed that all things under Heaven, the myriad creatures, that is to say all life, should be loved equally. Here Hui Tzu is coming close to the universal one-ness and origin role of the Tao which the *Tao Te Ching* started to explore. As Chapter 33 of the *Chuang Tzu* says, 'Hui Shih tried to introduce a more magnanimous view of the world and to enlighten the rhetoricians.' However, in the same chapter Chuang Tzu mocks Hui Shih's philosophical efforts, likening them to a mosquito or gnat in terms of their significance. Of more interest for us is his comment that 'if he had only shown greater respect for the Way, he would have come nearer being right.'

At times we catch sight of a very real personality in the stories about Chuang Tzu contained in the book. One of the most moving is his comments about the death of Hui Tzu, a death from which he seems never to have fully recovered.

'Chuang Tzu was once passing the grave of Hui Shih. He turned to his followers and said: "There was once a plasterer who used to ask his friend a stonemason, to strike off the little bits of plaster, no thicker than a fly's wing, that got onto his nose. The stonemason would swing his axe and the bit of plaster was gone, and the nose was not damaged and the plasterer never flinched. The Prince of Sung, having learnt of this, asked the stonemason to come and perform this feat before him. The stonemason replied: "It is true that I can perform this feat with an axe. Sadly the body which I used to work on is dead." Since the Master's death, I also have been without suitable material to work on. I have no-one left with whom to argue."'

(*Chuang Tzu*, Chapter 24.)

So we can begin to see that Chuang Tzu liked a good argument and was a man of strong attachments. But if there is one phrase which encapsulates his teachings it is that of individual freedom. The whole book shifts us away from the earnest kingly advice of the *Tao Te Ching*, the manual of leadership, towards the more traditional image of the Taoist sage as being the recluse, the one who rejected power, authority and position as illusion and as dangerous. The story given from Ssu-ma Ch'ien earlier, captures something of this rejection of power and authority. One of the most famous stories about Chuang Tzu gives us an insight into his attitude towards conventional thinking. Chuang Tzu loved taking events and giving them a thought-provoking twist. By doing so he is trying to free us from conventional ideas and patterns of behaviour; he is trying to get us to see deeper and to break the bounds of convention. This Way lies freedom.

When Chuang Tzu's wife died, Hui Tzu came to visit him to express his condolences. Imagine his horror when he found Chuang Tzu sprawled out banging a pot and singing! Hui Tzu remonstrated with Chuang Tzu. Was this how to honour the one you have lived with and who brought up your children, he asked. Chuang Tzu replied that at first he had been distressed like anyone else. But then he sat and thought about her.

I looked back to her beginning and the time before she was born. Not just then but the time before she had a body. Not only when she had had a body but the time before she had a spirit. From a time of astonishing mystery a transformation took place and she had a spirit. Another transformation and she had a body. One more change and she was born. Now there has been yet another change and she is dead. It is like the seasons. Spring, summer, autumn and winter. She is now going to lie down quietly in a large hall. If I followed her crying and weeping it would show that I have understood nothing about fate. That is why I stopped.'

(Chuang Tzu, Chapter 18.)

Death, in any society, is fraught with taboos. In Chinese traditional society, with its belief in ancestors and its rituals of death, this was even more so the case. Thus Chuang Tzu's attitude would have seemed even more shocking to his contemporaries than to us. Let us just look at one more story about death which he tells, to complete this picture.

'There were four friends, Messrs Ssu, Yo, Li and Lai. Together they wished to search for truth while recognizing that language could not help them. One day Mr Lai fell ill. It was obvious that he lay at death's door. His family gathered around him crying and weeping. Suddenly Mr Li appeared and chased them all away saying "Hush, don't disturb the process of change." Leaning against the door, Mr Li speculated upon what would become of Mr Lai. "How extraordinary the Creator of Life is. What is going to be made from you next? Where will you go? Will you be made into the liver of a rat, or perhaps into the arms of an insect?"'

(Chuang Tzu, Chapter 6.)

CHUANG TZU – THE THINKER

Chuang Tzu constantly tries to break down the reader's idea that change is bad and that if only we could get things straight, right and proper, then all would go well. In this vibrant model in which change is the essence of the Way, Chuang Tzu combines insights from Lao Tzu and from the *I Ching* – the Book of Change. He is also laying the foundations for the quest for immortality which saw flowing with the change as being a way in which life could continue.

It is in Chuang Tzu that we first seriously encounter the notion

54

of the immortal. The idea that there was a place or places where people lived but never died was current in China from at least the fifth century BC. Various rulers had sent expeditions to search for the islands of immortality or for the Kunlun mountains to the West. At the same time as the *Chuang Tzu* was being compiled, a number of expeditions set sail. As immortality became a major concern for later Taoism, it is perhaps important to just look at what Chuang Tzu said about the idea.

Chuang Tzu talks about the Perfected Person or Man. Usually he refers to someone living in antiquity. Such a person is able to defy all natural hazards such as water or fire. He can live on nothing but air and travel through the skies at will. Ultimately of course, he is able to defy death itself. In Chuang Tzu's descriptions the Perfected Man is a veritable bridge between Heaven and Earth. At one level we are back into the terms used about the shamans – and Chuang Tzu has a number of shamans appear in his stories, not always very favourably.

In Chuang Tzu, the Perfected Man is cosmic in his significance and role. He is the symbol of complete freedom because he is completely at one with, and able to move through, the universe. As such it is very questionable as to whether Chuang Tzu meant him to be taken seriously! By that I mean that the Perfected Man comes to be a symbol of the Perfected Way for humanity, indeed for all life. He is an archetype rather than a model we can imitate. Later generations interpreted these descriptions to be basic outlines of formulas for attaining immortality. I suspect that Chuang Tzu would have written something rather humorous about such an idea. In all the descriptions, we encounter a personification of freedom, not a manual on how to be immortal. For instance, listen to these excerpts from one description in Chapter 2 of the *Chuang Tzu*.

'The Perfected Man is pure spirit. He does not feel either the heat of the burning heaths nor the cold of the vast waters. He is not frightened by the lightning which can split open mountains, nor by the storms that can whip up the ocean. Such a person rides the clouds as though they were his carriage and treats the sun and moon as if they were his horses. He wanders across the Four Seas and the neither life nor death concerns him, nor is good or evil of any interest to him.'

In other places Chuang Tzu draws upon one or other of these features when describing actual sages such as Lieh Tzu. Lieh Tzu is recorded as being able to ride the clouds. But at no point does Chuang Tzu say that the Perfected Man is related to any actual human being. This is why I suspect that Chuang Tzu was setting up a cosmic man to act as an archetype for perfect freedom, not as a model for human achievement. Furthermore, when Chuang Tzu does discuss methods used for immortality, he often does so with his tongue firmly in his cheek. However, whatever Chuang Tzu may have thought has long since ceased to matter as Taoism developed these ideas for its mystical processes of immortality and sageship, as we shall see later.

What Chuang Tzu does stress is the ways in which one ought not to start on the path to wisdom. He offers very 'Taoist' advice on the essential nature of the quest for freedom and for meaning. Take for instance this nice incident told in Chapter 23. A man called Nan-jung Chu came to see the sage Lao Tzu hoping that he could help him deal with his worries and anxieties. As soon as Lao Tzu saw him, he said, 'Why have you come with such a vast crowd of people?' Nan-jung Chu spun round to see who he was talking about. Needless to say, Lao Tzu was referring to the host of worries and concerns that the man had brought with him.

Chuang Tzu also introduces us to the idea of how long, difficult and arduous it will be to seek for freedom and understand the Way. When he is discussing Lieh Tzu, he tells us that Lieh Tzu spent three years initially studying with his Master. At the end of this time he could no longer distinguish between truth and falsehood. At this point his Master deigned to notice him for the first time. After five years he began to see the difference between truth and falsehood. His Master smiled at him. After seven years, he managed to rid his mind entirely of the notion of truth or falsehood and for the first time he was invited to sit beside his Master. Finally, after nine years he saw that inside and outside were the same; that truth and falsehood were not an issue; he felt his physical body falling apart and becoming irrelevant and he found he could travel with the wind, blown along like a leaf.

Here is the classic description of the Taoist training – and indeed some have claimed that the Ch'an (Known in Japan as Zen) Buddhist techniques have been derived in part from Chuang Tzu's texts. The Way that cannot be spoken can only be appreciated in silence and through the collapse of rational thought. This is the secret of Chuang Tzu and it is perhaps best captured in his story about his dream of being a butterfly (see page 7).

It is time now to look at what Chuang Tzu has to offer to the notion of Tao and thus to see if he really can be described as a true 'Taoist'. It is important to realise that Chuang Tzu never defines the Tao. This would go against his belief in the limitations of such definitions, indeed, their ability to make one stumble. Chuang Tzu makes it clear that he himself has limited ability to express anything about the Tao. 'I have travelled through it this way and that, but I still only know where it begins. I have roamed around as I wished within its mind-bending vastnesses. I know how to get there but I do not know where they end.'

For Chuang Tzu the Tao is the ultimate both cosmically and in terms of the underlying unity of all life. Being the source from which all life has come, by which it is nourished and through which it will return, it is also the very essence of life. Chuang Tzu goes further than Lao Tzu in exploring the way in which the Tao is all things and thus is the unity of all things. To understand the Tao is to understand the sameness of everything. This is well captured in Chapter 2.

'If you look at a little stalk or point to a giant pillar, see a leper or the beautiful Hsi-shih, notice things which are funny and dubious or things hideous and strange, the Tao makes them all into one.'

The Tao is also a method for Chuang Tzu – the Way to sagehood or even further. Such people can have the talent of a sage, but not the Tao of a sage, while others can have the Tao of a sage but not the skills of a sage. In other words, the Tao becomes an awareness which heightens that which has already been experienced and understood, or indeed vice versa. But this needs to be put into a very clear context. Chuang Tzu makes it plain that anyone relying upon anything deemed useful by the world's standards is never going to approach the Tao. It is only by abandoning the rational models of understanding that true understanding comes. To the outside world, such practices and reasoning will seem pure folly. To illustrate this Chuang Tzu tells of an old tree.

'Carpenter Shih was travelling with his assistant through the state of Ch'i. One day they reached a village called Crooked Shaft. There in the centre of the village stood a vast serrated oak. It was so broad it could shelter two or three thousand oxen. It was a hundred spans in circumference and its lowest branches were eighty feet above the ground. Carpenter Shih didn't give it more than one glance but walked on past. His assistant stood dumbfounded before the great oak and then ran to catch up with Carpenter Shih. The assistant exclaimed that he had never seen such a wonderful tree in all his life, yet his master had walked straight past. Why was this?

'Carpenter Shih dismissed it out of hand. It is a useless tree he said because nothing could be made from such wood. This is why it has been around for so long.

That night Carpenter Shih dreamed that the tree appeared to him and lectured him. It demanded to know by what standards Shih was judging it. "Are you comparing me to those useful trees such as the cherry, the apple, the pear, the orange, the citron and the rest of those fruit bearing trees and bushes? As soon as their fruit appears they are torn apart and abused," said the tree. "No," said the tree. "I have been trying for a long time to be useless! It nearly killed me, but I have done it! If I had been of any use, do you think I would have lasted this long? Why do you then call me worthless? You, after all are a worthless man about to die – how do you know I am a worthless tree?"'

(Chuang Tzu, Chapter 4.)

For Chuang Tzu, the idea of finding an answer to the question, 'what is Tao?' is not only ridiculous, it is also to ask the wrong question. Therefore we shall have to be satisfied with the fact that for Chuang Tzu, the Tao is both immanent – when asked 'Where is this thing you call the Tao?' he replied 'Tao is in an ant, a blade of grass, a tile, a pile of dung' (Chapter 22) – and transcendent – 'Tao . . . is trunk and root, both together. Before Heaven or Earth existed, it had already been in existence for all eternity . . . it gives life to Heaven and Earth.' (Chapter 6). It is both an ultimate and a path; an unknowable end and a discernible beginning, but only if you abandon the way of the world. It can guide rulers, but it also confounds those who seek to rule. The sage knows how to rule or act with the Tao. The Perfected Man offers the supreme symbol of the unity of all in Tao and the sage points the Way. The wise men of old gained the Tao, and the greater Masters such as Lieh Tzu reached a stage of being able to join and flow with the Tao. But to ask more of Chuang Tzu in terms of description, definition or the way to the Way would be to invite the sound of his laughter ringing down the ages.

His thoughts encourage us to classify him as a Taoist though the phrase would probably have struck him as presumptuous and it is unlikely that he would have used it of himself. If anything, Chuang Tzu is the archetypal jester/fool who mocks the conventions to show the way to a higher understanding and experience. As such, it is perhaps sad that so many people have failed to laugh with Chuang Tzu and have instead tried to treat every word of his as a coded message. The vitality of Chuang Tzu is that even today his stories are still funny, pertinent and, most of all, revealing.

LIEH TZU

Finally, in our voyage through the great figures whose ideas coalesced into Taoism, we come to Lieh Tzu. As we have seen, Chuang Tzu knew him as someone who had achieved such a state of union with the Tao that he could ride the clouds. For Chuang Tzu, Lieh Tzu was the example par excellence of the sage and he used him to show how the sage arrived at his sagacity.

We know virtually nothing about Lieh Tzu from sources other than the *Lieh Tzu*. Apart from the fact that Chuang Tzu mentions him, we have no other details about him from sources outside the book which bears his name. Indeed, some commentators have doubted whether he existed at all and have claimed Chuang Tzu invented him to make a point. However I feel that the details given about Lieh Tzu, and the use of the specific phrase 'rode the clouds' means that Chuang Tzu is working from an already existing tale about someone called Lieh Tzu. As readers will have now gathered, Tzu simply means Master, so the name tells us nothing much. We do not know where he was born, nor where he died, though Chuang Tzu has a story about how he died which is given at the very end of this chapter. According to the *Lieh Tzu* itself, he lived in the wilds of the state of Cheng, at a place called Pu-t'ien. He was a recluse whom nobody noticed for many decades. A true sage removed from the world, he studied under a Master called Hu Tzu, along with his friend, Po-hun Wu-jen.

Lieh Tzu was obviously a figure about whom and around whom stories gathered. These were gradually collected together, presumably by the followers who are mentioned in the book, and were compiled into a book bearing his name. This book is the most recent of all the three books we have looked at. Scholarship is divided on when the book was written. Many Chinese writers believe it was during the second century BC, while most western scholars favour the third century AD. I find myself more convinced by the arguments for the second century BC – and even if this were not the case, most of the stories certainly obtained their basic shape around that time. Whatever the actual date, it immediately strikes the reader as being a less polished version of the style of the *Chuang Tzu*. It combines stories, jokes, tales and legends with reflection and thoughtful quotes. It lacks the sparkling wit and repartee of the *Chuang Tzu*, but its collection of stories are as good as many within the *Chuang Tzu*.

Like Chuang Tzu, Lieh Tzu sees the Tao as being the origin and the purpose of all life. Like Chuang Tzu, he also sees the Tao as immanent or all-pervading in life thus providing it with a unity. This is nicely brought out in the story of the outspoken twelve-year-old as told in Chapter 8.

Mr T'ien intended going on a long journey. To prepare for this he offered sacrifices to the gods of the road and gave a great feast for a thousand guests. When the dishes of fish and goose were brought round, Mr T'ien looked benignly upon them and said: 'How kind Heaven is to humanity. It provides the five grains and nourishes the fish and birds for us to enjoy and use.'

At this little piece of anthropocentrism, all the guests agreed; all, that is, except the twelve-year-old son of Mr Pao. He stepped forward and said: 'My Lord is wrong! All life is born in the same way that we are and we are all of the same kind. One species is not nobler than another; it is simply that the strongest and cleverest rule over the weaker and more stupid. Things eat each other and are then eaten, but they were not bred for this. To be sure, we take the things which we can eat and consume them, but you cannot claim that Heaven made them in the first place just for us to eat. After all, mosquitoes and gnats bite our skin, tigers and wolves eat our flesh. Does this mean Heaven originally created us for the sake of the mosquitoes, gnats, tigers and wolves?'

In the *Lieh Tzu* we again meet themes which are familiar from the *Chuang Tzu*. The Perfected Man is yet again presented as the perfection of all life through his fusion with the Tao. In the *Lieh Tzu* it is possible to see how the political sage of the *Tao Te Ching* has become fused with the symbolic Perfected Man of Chuang Tzu resulting in an odd mixture between the two. A case of being neither here nor there! At times Lieh Tzu combines descriptions of the sage or immortal undergoing his austere lifestyle, with terms which actually describe the Tao itself. In Chapter 2, called the Yellow Emperor, Lieh Tzu says this.

'Upon the Ku-ye mountains lives the Perfected Man. He breathes the winds and drinks the dew and does not eat the five grains. His mind is like a ceaseless spring, his body is like that of a youth. He does not know either intimacy nor love even though immortals and sages serve under him. He inspires no fear and is never angry – yet the ambitious and the careful work for him. He has no kindness nor generosity – yet those with him always have sufficient. He does not hoard nor save but he never goes without.'

The text goes on to say that yin and yang, the seasons, the planets and all of life is in harmony because of him.

Like Chuang Tzu, Lieh Tzu has been used to provide a manual for immortal training. Yet this is not what Lieh Tzu is writing about. He shares Chuang Tzu's lack of interest in the physical body, having a very similar attitude towards death.

Where Lieh Tzu is different from Chuang Tzu is in his attitude to, or rather use of, Confucius (K'ung). One entire chapter of the eight in the *Lieh Tzu*, is called K'ung Fu-tzu. In it Lieh Tzu uses K'ung to mock the hidebound Confucians of his own day. In this chapter K'ung's quest for the Tao is given a totally 'Taoist' meaning and through this he is able to deride the pretentions of the Confucians. Whereas Chuang Tzu sometimes mocked and sometimes praised K'ung, Lieh Tzu uses K'ung's ideas to emphasize the follies of the sort of reasoning that the Confucians were using in philosophical arguments. This gives us a very humble K'ung who is modesty itself! Not exactly the picture we have of K'ung from his own writings nor from the writings of his followers, but nevertheless interesting in reflecting both the fact that K'ung did concern himself with Tao and the fact that any book trying to impress in the cultural world of third to second century China had to have K'ung on its side.

THE TRUE STATE OF WISDOM

What Lieh Tzu does show us is how the idea of the hidden sage, the Taoist in the mountain retreat, the one who abandons all hold on normal life, is the one on the true Path. While his stories are not as finely tuned as Chuang Tzu's, he does put things rather well at times. In Chapter 2 he uses the example of a drunk to show what is the true state of wisdom.

'When a drunk is chucked off the cart, it doesn't matter how heavily he falls, he will not be killed. His bones and body are the same as any other person's, but he is not harmed like anyone else because of how he actually is. He has travelled in the cart without knowing it; he falls off without noticing; life and death, wonder and terror do not exist for him so he does not mind hitting the ground. Now, if this is true of a man whose wisdom comes as a result of drink, you can imagine what this would mean if the wisdom came from Heaven. The sage is caught up in Heaven and thus nothing can touch him.'

Lieh Tzu also stresses through many different stories, that those who wish to learn must start humbly and must progress stage by stage – not by questions but by patient observation, reflection and development. In Chapter 5, The Questions of T'ang, Lieh Tzu quotes an old poem to illustrate this.

'The son of a good bow maker
begins by making baskets.
The son of a good blacksmith
begins by making tools.'

The *Lieh Tzu*, much more than the *Chuang Tzu*, tries to give stories and teachings which will help someone seeking to find the Way. In doing so it naturally strives not to say what the Way is but to indicate the path towards it. In the *Lieh Tzu* we can see the development of beliefs from the *Tao Te Ching*'s collection of insights into reality, language, meaning and statescraft, through the wit and anarchistic insights of Chuang Tzu, to the beginnings of what we know today as Taoism. It now remains for us to see what happened over the next few centuries and to see how the old shamanistic traditions began to come back into play, drawing the words of the philosophers whom later generations called Taoists into the practice of the *fang-shih*, shamanists and ordinary people of the day.

Before we leave him though, it might be fun to hear just one last story from Chuang Tzu. It relates to the tension which we are about to examine between the philosophical thoughts of these writers and the divination practices which are the hallmark of so much popular Taoism, and especially its shamanistic roots. In Chapter 7, Chuang Tzu tells the following story about Lieh Tzu.

In Cheng there lived a shaman called Chi Hsien. He was very skilful in fortune-telling and divination. People were dumbfounded by his skills and knowledge of the future. When Lieh Tzu went to see him and saw what he did, Lieh Tzu was bowled over and fell under his spell. Upon his return to his own Master, Hu Tzu, Lieh Tzu told him that the shaman's powers were more impressive than even Hu Tzu's teachings about the Way. The shaman's teachings seemed to Lieh Tzu to be a perfection of the Way.

Hu Tzu was not exactly pleased at this! 'I have shown you all the external manifestations of the Tao but nothing of its true essence – so how can you think you have mastered my teachings of the Tao. It is like a flock of hens. Fine, but without a cock there can be no chicks!' So saying, he told Lieh Tzu to bring the shaman to meet him.

Now the shaman was obviously good at physiognomy, an art which was just coming into prominence at the time of the third to fourth centuries BC. So the shaman came and met Hu Tzu. As they left the room, the shaman said to Lieh Tzu how sorry he was to see that Hu Tzu was about to die. 'He will be dead by this time next week,' said the shaman. Lieh Tzu was horrified and ran back to his Master weeping.

Hu Tzu soon calmed him down. 'Don't worry' he said, 'I had on the Appearance of Earth – still and quiet, nothing moved, nothing emanating. He probably saw me as close to death. Bring him to see me again.'

So, the next day, Lieh Tzu brought the shaman again. On their way out, the shaman turned to Lieh Tzu and said, 'What good fortune I came to see him. He is going to live now for I saw life coming back again.'

Lieh Tzu reported this to Hu Tzu. Hu Tzu said: 'I appeared to him this time as Heaven and Earth – the nameless and non-substantial

63

but operating, breathing from my very depths.' And once again Lieh Tzu was instructed to bring the shaman back.

The next day, the shaman came away very perplexed and said that there was no way he could use his physiognomy skills on Hu Tzu unless he agreed to settle down. So, Hu Tzu told Lieh Tzu to bring the shaman again.

The next day, the shaman entered Hu Tzu's room again. But he got no further. With a cry of terror, the shaman turned and ran. Although Lieh Tzu ran as fast he could after him, he never caught up with him. Returning to Hu Tzu, he asked what had happened. 'This time,' said Hu Tzu, 'I appeared as the yet to be born from the origin. I came at him as nothing, wriggling and twisting, nothing definable, weaving and bending all over the place. That is why he ran!'

Lieh Tzu was so ashamed he went off home and for three years he did nothing except keep house for his wife and tend the pigs. He gradually cleared his mind and eventually achieved unity with the Tao. In this way, he died.

4 · THE BEGINNINGS OF RELIGIOUS TAOISM

In the year 221 BC China suffered the greatest shock to its self-perception and self-image that ever occurred. In one fell swoop most of the pillars of meaning by which China had been upheld, were smashed and broken. Elaborate codes and rituals were discarded and a wholesale assault was launched upon the very heart of ancient China. What happened?

CH'IN SHIH HUANG TI

In the year 246 BC a young boy called Chao Cheng ascended the throne of the Kingdom of Ch'in. This most western of the kingdoms had arisen during the Warring States period and was numbered along with seven other states. In 256 BC Chao Cheng's father had conquered the nearby state of Chou. When Chao Cheng came to the throne there were six other states still thriving. By the year 221 BC, he had conquered every single one of them and had a standing army of some one million men. In the year 221, having united all of traditional China, he was declared the Emperor. However, Chao Cheng was not just any Emperor; his formal title was Ch'in Shih

65

Huang Ti, meaning the First Ch'in Yellow Emperor. In taking such a title he was deliberately usurping the title of the most famous and wise of the ancient Emperors, Huang Ti. He was also using a title which had become a title for a god. By using this title Chao Cheng clearly announced that he was ushering in a new era. In his victory proclamations he claimed that the Ch'in Dynasty would last for ten thousand generations. As we shall see, this proved to be somewhat of an exaggeration. Yet, in one way at least, he might not have been far wrong. The name 'China' comes from the name of his dynasty – such was the impression his reign had, not just on China, but far beyond its borders.

To the peoples of China the shock of conquest and dictatorial unity was terrible. It threw all the philosophical schools into turmoil as all normative guidelines were broken and threatening new patterns began to be established. Ch'in Shih Huang Ti founded and bloodily kept together a new centralized system of counties and districts. By doing so and appointing governors, he was able to maintain a tight control over his people. He sent armies down into the lands to the south of traditional China, reaching as far as modern-day Vietnam. To the north he built large stretches of the Great Wall, and linked up small sections which had been built by the various states over the centuries.

Near modern day Sian, he built a massive palace, of which more later. Today, outside China, he is best remembered for his vast tomb with the ranks of terracotta soldiers discovered only in the last few years. Inside China he became to later generations the personification of all that was evil in government and all that was antithetical to traditional China. It is not without significance that Mao Tse-tung spoke highly of Ch'in Shih Huang Ti as a role model, for until the Communist Revolution, nothing so traumatic as the unification under Ch'in ever happened again.

Ch'in Shih Huang Ti undertook fundamental steps which made it possible for China to be turned into an empire capable of being held together. His administrative reforms were remarkable and present day China still owes a lot to him for his organization of counties and districts and the basic structure of government. He was also the first man to order a systematization of the written language. Under his rule the Chinese written language was simplified and unified, making it possible to communicate right across China, regardless of local differences in pronunciation. However, all this was possible only because he ruled ruthlessly and brutally. In particular, he came to realize that he could not afford to have any other ways of thinking survive, thus he had to destroy alternative ways of ruling, philosophizing and behaving. To do this, in 213 BC he ordered that all the ancient books be destroyed. All histories, books of the classics, wisdom writings and so forth were to be surrendered to the government and burnt. The only books spared this were 'useful' ones such as those on divination like the *I Ching*, medicine such as the Yellow Emperor's book and on agriculture. All others were ruthlessly sought out and burnt. Any scholar found trying to hide them was ordered to be killed. It is said that three hundred scholars, mostly Confucians, were buried alive. It is impossible to know quite how much was lost for ever at this time. Certainly, China suffered a cultural destruction which easily compares to the destruction of the Great Library at Alexandria.

THE SAGE EMPEROR

This man, who brought tyranny and cultural devastation to China, was also deeply interested in what was later to be one of the core elements of Taoism – the quest for immortality. Indeed, Ch'in Shih Huang Ti saw himself as being almost the classic Lao Tzu ruler. He certainly used many terms which are now familiar to us. Here are a few quotes from the records of Ssu-ma Ch'ien from the stone inscriptions which Ch'in Shih Huang Ti set up around the country:

'In the twenty-eighth year of his reign
A new age is inaugurated by the Emperor;
Rules and measures are rectified,
All living things set in order,
Human affairs made clear
And there is harmony between fathers and sons.'

'All under Heaven is at peace to the glory of the imperial ancestral temple. The Emperor carries out the True Tao and practises virtue (te), living up to his exalted title.'

'The Sovereign Emperor came to the throne. . . .
His obedient subjects remember his achievements, trace them from the start and celebrate his virtue (te).

67

Beneath his wide sway all things find their place, all is decreed by
law;
Great and manifest, his virtue is handed down to ages yet to come,
to be followed without change.
The sage Emperor who has pacified all under heaven is tireless in
his rule.'

Our interest in the 'sage Emperor' is at two levels. Firstly, he was
fascinated in immortality and in certain beliefs about the gods and
about alchemy which were later to emerge as the hallmarks of
popular Taoism. Secondly, he set in motion a series of profound
questions about the meaning of individual life, resulting in the rise
of religious Taoism with its answers to the question of individual
fate, meaning and purpose. As such, in both activities, he drew
deeply upon the shamanistic practices which, as we saw in Chapter
2, had continued in an unofficial way even under the Confucians.
Now, fusing with ideas developed by the philosophical school of
Taoism, they began to take on a new life in the years after the Ch'in
dynasty: in that very period when we can begin to talk about there
being a self-conscious Taoist movement.

THE QUEST FOR IMMORTALITY

Let us start with the quest for immortality with which Ch'in Shih
Huang Ti was obsessed. He had been told that there were three
magic islands in the ocean where the immortals lived, so he built
and provisioned a fleet to go and search for them. To staff his fleet
he chose thousands of virgins and young men and sent them off to
find immortality. No-one knows what the ship-loads of virgins and
young men found, but whatever it was, they never returned, even
though the Emperor would spend hours staring out to sea in the
hope of spotting them!

His next venture was to send three shamans and scholars to search
for the elixir of life. Similar expeditions were sent out periodically,
but to no avail. Ch'in Shih grew anxious. To reassure him, one Lu,
a magician/shaman of considerable skills, tried to explain what was
going wrong.

'Our search for magic fungus, rare herbs and immortals has come
to nothing. It seems some sinister influence was against us. It is my
sincere opinion that you would be well advised to change your

quarters secretly from time to time in order to avoid evil spirits: for in their absence some pure being will come. For subjects to know their sovereign's whereabouts detracts from his divinity. A pure being is one who cannot be wet by water or burned by fire, who rides on the clouds and air and endures as long as heaven and earth.'

(Ssu-ma Ch'ien)

The Emperor accordingly ordered that all his palaces be linked by covered walkways, thus making it possible for him to travel around without being seen. What is so interesting in this account from Ssu-ma Ch'ien, is the language that is used to describe the immortal. It is identical to that of Chuang Tzu when describing the Perfected Man. It is obvious that by the time of Ch'in Shih Huang Ti (c.220 BC) the descriptions in the Chuang Tzu were being taken literally rather than figuratively. The process of the Way to immortality rather than the Way of the immortals had begun.

For all his attempts, death eventually caught up with the Emperor and in the year 210 BC he died. His eleven years as Emperor of all China had transformed it, but his own dynasty only lasted a further four years! It was overthrown by the founder of the Han dynasty and thus China began one of its most illustrious eras.

HUANG-LAO – EARLY TAOISM

The reverberations of what had happened continued to echo around the Empire. This brings us to the second of the major effects of Ch'in Shih Huang Ti's reign. Before his time, the vast majority of the people were quite content to find immortality and meaning through their descendants. The idea of individual survival and meaning after death was not one which was very widespread before the Han dynasty. The individual found his or her meaning through being part of the community of the clan/family. Prior to the first century BC, it would have struck most Chinese as odd to think about their own existence after death. After all, through the ancestor rites your name was remembered for many generations. You were believed to continue to be part of the wider family, both physical and spiritual. Quite what this entailed or meant was never very clear. It arose from the shamanistic world view whereby the physical world was but a mirror of the spiritual world.

If you turned to Confucian thinking for solace as an individual, there was little there for you. K'ung himself had dismissed speculation about life after death on the grounds that it was hard enough to deal with the current reality, never mind the reality of another world! The rigid hierarchical structure of the filial piety system meant that your place in the world was clearly delineated by convention and thus extistentialist doubts were really not relevant. It is perhaps hard for us to appreciate the extent to which people's identity was caught up and subsumed in the family. The family, the ruler and the hierarchy of male and female, elder and younger, ruler and ruled, was there and was eternal, fixed for ever – indeed part of the cosmic order. How could this ever change?

Then Ch'in Shih Huang Ti burst upon the scene and showed how temporal, fragile and changeable everything was. In eleven years he turned China upside down and his reforms were continued under the Han dynasty – for the simple reason that they worked. However, in the process the small kingdoms with their clans disappeared from the scene. The old learning was attacked and destroyed. Suddenly everything under Heaven and on Earth seemed much more vulnerable to human action than had previously been thought possible. For the individual, old certainties which had never been questioned turned into structures which could be broken, destroyed or, at the least, substantially changed. From this situation arose, over a long period of time, a persistent questioning as to the place and relevance of the individual in society. Questions which for the vast majority of people had never been there before. It is not without significance that it was around this time that the first major commentaries on the *I Ching* were written, with their emphasis on constant change being the nature of reality.

Allied with these questions came the desire for a greater assurance of individual continuance after death than just ancestor worship could provide. Furthermore, it began to be important that the individual should be assured of his or her relationship with the gods both in this world and the afterlife. Whereas previously the shaman had functioned as the link between communities and the spiritual world, it now became increasingly important to individuals that they should have some means of control or ability to ward off the more malignant of the spiritual forces.

However, there were also deeper questions being raised. The concept of the yin and yang, the idea of a balance between forces within which humanity played a vital role, developed from being a largely kingly function to being one in which all people shared to some degree. This meant that whereas previously the people looked to the king or emperor to exonerate them before Heaven, now the individual began to feel responsible. So illness, suffering, disaster and the like were no longer seen as being beyond the individual's control. Now the individual could be held responsible for such events having happened, for having disturbed the natural order, the Tao. As such, it began to matter to people what forces were arraigned against them in the spirit world and it became important to find out how to control or appease them.

It is one of the most remarkable things about the Early Han period that it is in this era that we find the first major and popular manifestations of divination at a folk level, of physiognomy, of *feng shui* (geomancy) and other such practices. It is as if there were a great longing to know and to be in touch with the spiritual world. It is no exaggeration to say that during the period from 208 BC to the end of the first century AD, there was a virtual explosion in religious practices, beliefs, gods, deities, magic, divination and the like. Into this ferment of activity seeped various ideas from the great philosophers. Thus we find folk beliefs beginning to take shape about the Perfected Man being an actual achievable goal for ordinary humans. We find academic notions of the divine, of the natural forces, becoming personified and venerated.

Even more remarkable, we find the great philosophers being deified. K'ung, who had virtually denied the relevance of the spiritual and of the gods, was busy being worshipped by the end of the first century BC and in AD 59 the Emperor formalized this by decreeing that sacrifices could and indeed should be offered to K'ung. At the same time Lao Tzu and the Yellow Emperor were themselves being worshipped as the manifestations of the Tao. Indeed, at this time what we call Taoism was actually known as Huang-Lao. Certainly by around 100 BC, there were at least three major cosmic deities being worshipped by such followers, Lao Tzu, the Yellow Emperor and a deity known as T'ai I – meaning the Great Unity – which is of course the philosophers' term for the ultimate understanding of the Tao as the foundation, origin and pre-origin of all existence. This was developed even further in that Lao Tzu and the Yellow Emperor came to be seen as human manifestations, avatars or incarnations of the Supreme Unity and were accordingly worshipped as such.

LAO TZU AS THE PRIMAL MAN

An even more remarkable transformation had taken place by the third century AD, when we find Lao Tzu depicted as the primal man who gave physical life to the planet. This is in fact an adaptation of the older myth about P'an Ku who carved the earth to the shape it has today, but it was only when he gave his life in the struggle to mould the world that life came to the earth. The myth continues in traditional style that P'an Ku's blood became the rivers; his hair became the trees and forests; his bones became the rocks. When the Taoists made Lao Tzu into a latter day P'an Ku they went a bit further. His left eye became the sun and his right eye the moon. His beard created the stars, his bones the rocks, his flesh gave rise to the four-footed animals, his belly became the sea – and so on. We have moved a long way from the human writer of the fifth century BC!

THE TAO TE CHING AS GUIDEBOOK

The *Tao Te Ching* had not fared much better. It was revered as the central text of the emerging 'Taoists' but not in a way which perhaps Lao Tzu would have recognized – certainly not in a way that Chuang Tzu or Lieh Tzu would have approved. The *Tao Te Ching* had become a spiritual/ethical book, credited with offering teachings about how to live your daily life. It had also become a charm, used to ward off evil spirits (which with the breakdown of the old shamanist role and the growth of psychological angst, had become fearful forces against which humans had little defence). To give you some idea of the way the *Tao Te Ching* became a guidebook, let me just give you the best-known lines of commentary on the first lines of Chapter 1.

> *The Tao that can be followed*, that is to eat good things in the morning; *the Way that is not eternal*, that is to go to the toilet in the evening . . . *Mysterious and yet more mysterious*: that is the nose and the mouth.' (Quoted in *Taoism and Chinese Religion* by Henri Maspero, translated by FA Kierman Jr, University of Massachusetts Press, 1981.)

72

TAOISM AS A FAITH

I have tried to indicate throughout that we need to see the Lao Tzu school and its heirs such as Chuang Tzu and Lieh Tzu as but part of the forces which came together to be called Taoism. The role of the shamanistic world view both in shaping the idea of the Tao as the ultimate, and as carrying forward an active and popular vision of the spirit world's relationship to the material world, was one of the other great forces helping to create 'Taoism'. To this must be added a third belief and that is the desire for immortality. I do not believe that Chuang Tzu thought in terms of the Perfected Man being an achievable goal for ordinary people, nor even for the sage. I believe that he was using that term to describe an absolute, as I have said in the section on Chuang Tzu. But it is obvious that both he and Lieh Tzu were aware of those who sought immortality and while they both keep an edge of scepticism, they are nevertheless prepared to accept that it may be possible. Chuang Tzu described Lieh Tzu in classical immortal terms.

We have also seen that rulers such as Ch'in Shih Huang Ti were very familiar with the concept of immortality. It seems that whilst he used language which echoes the 'Taoist' philosopher's language, Ch'in Shih Huang Ti was also drawing upon a tradition which was wider than just that found within the 'Taoist' philosophers. Where it came from it is impossible to say. It may be that it began with Lao Tzu's Perfect Man which then became a goal for rulers and eventually became a goal for all humans. But I suspect that we are in fact dealing with yet another force which flowed into the mixture which we now call Taoism. There have been many attempts to see formulas and prescriptions for immortality practices as being contained or hinted at within the *Tao Te Ching*, the *Chuang Tzu* and the like. It may be that such hints exist, but there is also no serious doubt that ideas of immortality were circulating quite freely well beyond the bounds of these schools.

It is important to realize that it is only when the three main streams – shamanism and the *fang-shih*, Lao Tzu and the schools of Chuang Tzu etc and the quest for immortality in its popular non-ruler/sage model – come together that we can really talk about there being such a thing as 'Taoism'. Prior to that there were streams of thought flowing to some degree independently; to some degree already asborbing and being absorbed by the others; whilst a parallel but independent stream of Confucian thought was also emerging. Thus when we start to talk, as we now can, about Taoism as a self-conscious faith, we are talking about a dynamic relationship between these various strands. This is important because many people who have read the *Tao Te Ching* without any understanding of its context or use in China, often feel profoundly disturbed when they encounter Taoism as a faith. This has been the case almost ever since the West encountered China. Thus it is that many have attacked religious Taoism, or what I would prefer to call Taoism per se, calling it a corruption of the purity of philosophical Taoism. This, however, is unfair to Taoism; it is rather like saying that democracy is too good for the likes of political parties to mess around with. It is an unrealistic and ultimately meaningless statement. So it is with the claim that pure Taoism degenerated into religious Taoism. To start with, the philosophical teachers never saw themselves as 'Taoists' in the first place. Secondly, if 'pure' Taoism ever existed as such, it certainly has not done so for some seventeen to eighteen hundred years. Thirdly, Taoism as a self-conscious faith was always a mix of these different streams, so it itself has not 'degenerated'.

Unfortunately, the West has often found it easier to pick up another culture's books and read them than it has been willing to explore the origins, the meaning in context and the challenge of very different models of reality and of life. This has meant that a rather romanticized vision of Taoism has become very common in the West. I do not doubt that it is in itself a valid western search after understanding. However, it often bears about as much resemblance to Taoism as lived and loved by the Chinese for two thousand years, as pacifism does to Hitler!

With the three streams merging we need to look at what each contributed to the melting pot to form Taoism and what this gave to the faith itself.

5 · FROM FIGHTERS TO FABLES

In late 1927, on Dragon and Tiger Mountain in the province of Kiangsi, a dynasty was deposed from its ancestral home. A Communist section of the Nationalist Army had broken off and was on its way to the coast to join the first Chinese soviet at Hailufeng, north of Canton, founded by the remarkable P'eng P'ai. En route they attacked Dragon and Tiger Mountain. The ruler of the mountain, the Celestial Master, T'ien Shih, escaped and fled from his ancestral home. Meanwhile, the troops smashed thousands of ancient jars and containers which they found stored in the vast temple complexes. In doing so they were undoing hundreds of years of work by the Celestial Masters. And, according to the faithful, they released thousands of the most evil demons, spirits and ghosts into the world again. Our first exploration into Taoism as a lived popular faith takes us into the extraordinary story of this mountain and the hereditary line of Changs, the T'ien Shih, the Celestial Masters of Taoism.

THE T'IEN SHIH

By the time of the Late Han, the second century AD, many of the forces which were to result in the formation of mass appeal Taoism were in place. The quest for a personal salvation and meaning had expanded, not least with the entry of Buddhism into the field of religious competition. The old shamanist magic, exorcism and divination was slipping away from them, but had as yet to find a new role or more socially acceptable practitioner. Meanwhile, the great Han dynasty, which had ruled for over three hundred years virtually unchallenged, was on its way out and all the signs of a coming time of tribulation were evident.

The Early Han dynasty was the one which arose to seize the prize of China away from the Ch'in dynasty. The Early Han is dated from 207 BC to AD 9. Then a short-lived dynasty erupted and ruled from AD 9 to AD 23. In AD 23 the Han dynasty reasserted itself and ruled on for another two hundred years. However, this Late Han dynasty never matched the skills of administration of the Early Han. In particular it began to develop an oppressive taxation system which was necessary to maintain the vast imperial court. By the middle of the second century AD revolts were breaking out across China as discontent was fuelled by avaricious taxation.

CHANG TAO LING

Into this changing scene was born Chang Ling. One story says he was born around the year AD 150 in the province of Szechwan. Another tells us he was born in AD 35. He claimed descent from the famous Chang Liang who in the year 206 BC had helped the Han dynasty come to power by using a powerful set of charms and magic to assist the troops in battle. It was claimed that these charms and the magic had been given to Chang Liang by Lao Tzu.

As a child Chang Ling was a genius. He could read and understand the *Tao Te Ching* by the time he was seven. By the time he was eight he had mastered *feng shui* (geomancy) and astrology. As a young man he displayed remarkable powers and authority. In particular he seems to have had tremendous healing powers, both for physical illnesses and for what we would now call psychological ailments. In many ways he resembles the old shamans or the *fang-shih*, but there was one vital difference. Chang Ling didn't just heal people, exorcise demons or preach powerfully. He also organized his followers into a movement. This had never been done in this way before by such a person.

Chang Ling's technique was quite simple but revolutionary. In the

Chang Tao Ling with demon-capturing charm

past, judging from accounts of writers such as Ssu-ma Ch'ien, a great
fang-shih might have a following in the sense of people coming to
see him, but he never tried to organize them into a specific group.
However, Chang Ling did so by two means. Firstly, he instituted a
standard payment for his treatment. Anyone who came seeking help
had to agree to pay five bushels of rice each year thereafter. As this is
quite a lot of rice, and the payment was guaranteed for many years,
this enabled Chang Ling to develop his second means of organizing
his followers into a specific 'faith' group. He created an increasingly
large organization upon these tithes. These fees were not just for
the sustaining of the shaman. Five bushels from an increasingly
large number of people meant that the healer could afford to pay
a growing hierarchy of followers, priests and other functionaries.
So unusual was this feature of his teachings, that Chang's groups
became known as the Five Bushels Sect.

Chang Ling claimed that Lao Tzu (who, we must remember, had
become well deified by now) had dictated to him the structure of
this organization of the followers. In what is now known as the
'Covenant of the Orthodox Unity with the Powers', Lao Tzu gave
Chang Ling the authority to establish twenty-four divisions of his
followers – along lines similar to the Christian diocese. Within these

77

twenty-four governances the faithful were organized, sustained and tithed. What is interesting about this Covenant (which tradition dates as having been given in 142 AD) is that it also gave Chang Ling power over the demonic forces as well as having his healing powers confirmed. In other words, it is this Covenant with Chang Ling which binds together the powers of the spirit world with the structures of the material world. In Chang Ling both meet and are organized and directed. The shaman has now become the controller of the fortunes of both the material and the spirit world.

It is difficult to know just what exactly Chang Ling taught. It would appear, from later stories, that he offered his followers a mixture of personal well-being based upon personal salvation and cleansing, along with various ideas of immortality. His means of healing is quite revealing. The person seeking healing was asked to write out all his or her sins and failures. Then, holding the paper above his or her head, he or she waded out into a river and was washed clean of all failures and shortcomings and cleansed of illness. This teaching was breaking new ground for it linked personal sins with illness and offered not just a physical healing but a psychological and spiritual one as well. Chang Ling, who took the title Chang Tao Ling to stress where his power and authority came from, was offering individuals a more radical and complete liberation than any other system had offered before. In a time of collapsing authority he was establishing a new order. At a time when Buddhism with its idea of salvation was becoming popular in certain circles, he provided Taoism with its own model of salvation. He was revolutionary.

Likewise, in the title he chose for himself, Celestial Master, he seems to be shifting the old shamanist role on to a new level. Instead of being the servant of the spiritual world, the intermediator, he claimed to be the controller of these forces. In later legends he is described as being the Perfected Man of Chuang Tzu and the Sage of the *Tao Te Ching*. In claiming that he was a Celestial Master, Chang Ling was making a vital theological assertion which then gave extra meaning to his healing and to his teachings. He was claiming that he could not only control Heaven, but also could confer the benefits of his control on others – mere mortals. Thus by participation in this sect, the ordinary person was offered a chance of salvation and fortune. This was no flash in the pan, no one night wonder. Here instead was a new reality breaking into the world, one which could rule over the forces of the spirit world and one who could steer you safely through them to wealth, security, well-being and personal happiness. All this for five bushel of rice a year!

With such a shift in the role of the leader figure, it is not surprising that Chang Ling soon had a quite considerable following and one which needed organizing. Even more interesting is the fact that he established a hereditary line. Now there was not only a group of followers; not only sufficient funds to pay for the institutes of religious life; not only a personal stake in Heaven for the ordinary people; but also a clear line of succession.

Before we proceed to look at what his son and grandson were able to build with this, we need to spend just a little more time with Chang Ling. In popular Taoism there is no more respected figure. Nor is there any other deity whose name is so constantly before the people. Chang Ling's religious title is Chang T'ien Shih and as such he is worshipped, venerated and called upon across the Chinese world today. In the almanacs, which are themselves a veritable storehouse of religious systems, pride of place is given to the charms of Chang Tao Ling. It is said that Chang Tao Ling was given by Heaven a great sword and seal, with which to keep the demons in control. By use of this sword and seal, and by the incantation of various charms and spells, he was able to capture or slay thousands of demons, thus freeing people from sickness and trouble. When he went to Heaven and became an immortal, he bequeathed his sword and his book of charms to his descendants. These charms are still in everyday use today. The power of Chang Tao Ling's name alone is supposed to be enough to frighten off the more mundane demons. In the almanacs you can find a range of charms drawing upon the authority of Chang Tao Ling, whose picture sits above them.

The sword of Chang Tao Ling was still visible at Dragon and Tiger Mountain until 1927 – or at least, what was claimed to be the sword. It was this which had been responsible for capturing the most evil demons who were imprisoned in the jars at the temple shrine of Dragon and Tiger Mountain.

Apart from his powers as an exorcist, Chang Tao Ling is renowned as the general in charge of all the troops of Heaven who sally forth to combat wicked dragons and demons. He also has ascribed to him no end of miracles and extraordinary skills, such as being able to split his self into two, so that one could entertain guests or teach while the other one went fishing!

Chang Tao Ling and his charms

In the persona of Chang Tao Ling we can clearly see the old shamanistic traditions fusing with the newer quest for personal meaning and well-being, whilst simultaneously drawing upon ideas which had come to be known as Taoist. With Chang Tao Ling, the three main streams which we have been following meet and mingle before flowing on.

CHANG HENG AND CHANG LU

What happened next is quite fascinating, for under Chang Tao Ling's grandson, Taoism developed one stage further, following the logic of both its shamanist roots and, at the same time, the idea of the sage of the *Tao Te Ching*. Chang Tao Ling died, or as the Taoists say, ascended to Heaven and became an immortal, somewhere around AD 160. His son, Chang Heng, took over as head of the faith, but apart from sustaining it, he contributed little to its development.

80

It is the grandson, Chang Lu, who took the next dramatic step. The Han dynasty was rapidly falling apart. Minor rebellions were erupting across China, but especially in its more remote provinces. The central Imperial Government was incapable of raising enough troops, so began to rely on local leaders and their forces. In AD 188 the local governor, Liu Yen, asked Chang Lu to lead an army to which Chang's own men were added, and to advance against Shu Ku, one of the rebels.

In seeking forces to complement his own, Chang asked for and received help from another head of a Taoist faith group. This was the remarkable Chang Hsiu. He had founded a group not dissimilar from that of Chang Tao Ling. He held healing ceremonies which were very specific. He locked up his patients and told them to reflect upon the sins which they had committed which had brought them to such ill-health. Once they had written all these down on three pieces of paper, the paper was destroyed in three different ways. One strip was taken to the top of a mountain and left for the wind and rain to dispose of, one strip was buried in the ground and one strip was cast into the waters. By doing so the patient was cured and, like Chang Tao Ling's followers, paid an annual fee of five bushels of rice. Like Chang Tao Ling, Chang Hsui had instituted a religious system of organization with a very detailed hierarchy which oversaw the lives and rituals of the faithful. It seems likely that he had actually copied Chang Tao Ling, for it is only in the 170's to 180's that we hear of Chang Hsiu – thirty years or more after Chang Tao Ling began in earnest.

The two armies of the two Changs combined and defeated the enemy. Then Chang Lu took things into his own hands. Aparently jealous of Chang Hsiu, he had him executed and merged Chang Hsiu's group with his own. Then, secure in a remote part of northern Szechwan, Chang Lu established a Taoist theocracy and declared his Taoist state to be independent of the Han Empire. This theocracy lasted thirty years and was a remarkable attempt to put into practice the teachings of the *Tao Te Ching* on rulership. It also has strong echoes back to the idealized rule of such semi-historical figures as the Yellow Emperor. But it was the *Tao Te Ching* which we know underpinned the rebellion, the rituals of healing and the theocracy. It was the Five Bushels sect which established the length of the *Tao Te Ching* at 5000 characters. It was compulsory for every household to own a copy of the *Tao Te Ching* and to study it daily.

Needless to say, many of the ideas in their official commentaries would have somewhat astonished Lao Tzu had he read them, but then as we have seen, this was how the *Tao Te Ching* was finding its very special place within the emerging faith of Taoism.

Under the rule of Chang Lu, the people lived in greater security than in many other parts of China at this time of dynastic collapse. Furthermore, Chang Lu instituted very benign laws, built free hostels on the roads for travellers, forbad the killing of animals for half the year, restricted alcohol and established a system of justice which was remarkable in its leniency towards criminals whom he believed were capable of being redeemed. The agricultural system was considerably improved, new roads built and stores of food established for the poor. All in all, his rule was quite an improvement on the rest of China.

However, Chang was also wise and when, after thirty years, it became obvious that the State was about to reinstate its authority, he surrendered and was able to live out his life in gentle and prosperous retirement. It was from this remarkable family that the hereditary Celestial Masters were descended. In later years they were given vast tracts of land over which they ruled like prince bishops, based on their mini-state at Dragon and Tiger Mountain.

YU CHI AND CHANG CHIAO

We now need to turn to what might look like the failure of a strand of religious Taoism but which was to have long-lasting consequences. You may have noticed by now that everyone associated with the early history of religious Taoism is called Chang. We are about to meet yet another Chang, but just to show it was not obligatory to be called Chang, we first encounter someone called Yu Chi. Yu Chi was another of these fascinating figures who combined the shamanistic with the medicinal and psychological. He was active around the same time as Chang Tao Ling and some claim that Chang Tao Ling was, in fact, one of his disciples. Yu Chi healed through ritual and charms but does not seem to have been so interested in establishing a religious group. Instead he followed the more traditional path of writing a book of his teachings. This book, much of which is sadly lost, was called the *T'ai p'ing Ch'ing ling Shu*, which means the Great Peace Book of the Pure Commands. An odd mixture of rituals, charms and sayings of the *fang-shih* about old and cosmological theories, it was to become the main formative book which brought about the emergence of the later sects of Taoism. Indeed, although only a shadow of its former self, the book heads the fifth section of the Taoist Canon of Scripture and its name is used as the title of the entire section.

The book laid the seeds for the later rebellion of Taoism. In the book, which Yu Chi claimed had been given to him by the gods, it was stated that Heaven, Earth and the rulers of humanity had all lost the true Way and abandoned the balance of yin and yang. Thus it was no longer necessary to obey the rulers but it was vital to restore proper order in the cosmos. This belief that the normal structures of society and of the cosmos had been breached was to lead to bloody insurrection a few decades later.

In the year AD 184 a new sixty year cycle of the the Chinese calendar began. In the Eastern provinces Chang Chiao had established a strong, militant and missionary Taoist healing sect. This sect was called the *T'ai p'ing Tao*, the Way of the Great Peace, and its central text, along with the *Tao Te Ching*, was Yu Chi's book. In a period of less than ten years its founder Chang Chiao had built up a formidable order. Using many of the ideas we have seen developed by the other Changs, he had established a well organized faith group. They converted, planned, prepared and waited. Then in 184, as the new sixty year cycle began, they erupted into rebellion. Their teachings claimed that the old Blue Heaven era (the Han dynasty) had ended. A new era was about to be born, the era of the Great Peace which would be part of the Yellow Heaven era. To initiate this new era, the troops of Chang Chiao wrapped yellow cloth around their heads, hence the title of the rebellion – the Yellow Turban Rebellion.

Despite promises of invulnerability to weapons and the reputed support of both the Yellow Emperor and Lao Tzu as the deities of Huang-Lao, the rebellion was eventually and brutally crushed. It is said that over 350,000 men took the field for militant Taoism, wearing their distinctive yellow headscarves. It took from AD 184 to the early years of the third century to put down the rebellion. The sect eventually abandoned rebellion and settled down to practise a less violent Taoism, eschewing armed rebellion. But the idea of armed rebellion, of the passing away of the mandate of rule from a dynasty and the idea of fighting Taoism, was far from dead and has continued to reappear down the centuries in Taoism, leading many emperors to view Taoism with more than a little suspicion. Here lie the origins of the later martial arts which were developed within the walls of Taoist monasteries and put to deadly use on the road and, more than occasionaly, in rebellion.

THE FIRST TAOIST CANON OF SCRIPTURES

Over the next few hundred years, sects and groupings within the popular level of organised Taoism grew and multiplied. It was a time of phenomenal expansion and of development of ideas. While it has been traditional for scholars to view the growth of 'religious' Taoism as basically containing more and more crass superstition, I feel, along with a growing number of other scholars, that this is grossly unfair. It was in fact a time of immense creativity and profound theological debates which manifested themselves in ritual, practice and texts.

In the year AD 471, the first Taoist Canon of Scriptures was compiled. It listed over 1200 books and drew from three main traditions which continue to this day. These three main traditions had by this time developed a concept of cosmic salvation which radically broke the bounds of the family-centred ideas of traditional Chinese thought; it had enfranchised an entire class of people, the poor and the workers, by offering not just personal salvation, but a role in cosmic salvation, and it had established one of the most complex systems of religious beliefs, deities and teachings that the world had ever seen. By anyone's measure, it was a remarkable achievement. Within all this were movements which focused on immortality through any number of esoteric methods, of which more later – martial schools, alchemistic traditions, philosophical drunks and humorists, as well as the usual scattering of charlatans, con-men, crooks and pious frauds which every religion attracts!

Before we look at the immortality schools, the alchemists and the philosopher/humorists, let us just look at the three main schools whose teachings were brought together to form the first Taoist Canon, for in them are many of the seeds of Taoism today.

THE CELESTIAL MASTER'S WAY

The first of these schools, though not in ultimate importance, is the Celestial Master's Way – sometimes referred to as the Orthodox Path

Way, from the name of Chang Tao Ling's revealed text. The greatest contribution of the successors of Chang Tao Ling and Chang Lu was that of the Taoist priest, the *tao shih*, with his local temple, his hierarchy leading to the Celestial Master, who was a sort of vague Archbishop figure, and the institution of the local 'parish' over whom the *tao shih* had responsibility. Linked to this, the sect also established the idea of the method of fees for the work of such specialists. It is this basic parochial, paid services model which has made it possible for Taoism to exist at such an all-pervasive level in China to this day. In contrast, the Buddhist monks had to rely upon alms, and were not central to the parish or even ritual life of the people. While a Buddhist monk or two might be invited to chant at birth ceremonies such as the First Month ceremony, at weddings or at funerals, all the ritual activities and necessary blessings and so on were always the province of the *tao shih*. That this is so is due in no small part to the Celestial Master's sect and the models which it pioneered. Also known as Meng-wei – The Auspicious Alliance – its head, the present Celestial Master, heir to the family and traditions of Chang Tao Ling, still lives in Taiwan where the parochial structure still exists to a considerable degree.

Taoist 'parish' priest

MAO SHAN

The second group is known as Mao Shan – Mao Mountain. The heart of this sect is their very strange but beautiful scriptures, known as the *Shang ch'ing* scriptures. Also unusual is the fact that their founder was a woman. Despite recent claims by writers anxious to respond to feminist critiques of religion, Taoism has always been a predominantly male religion – notwithstanding some of its finer teachings!

The founder of the Mao Shan sect was Wei Hua-ts'un who lived from AD 251 to 334. Trained as a libationer – that is a sort of 'bishop' within the *Meng-wei*/Celestial Master tradition – she married and raised a family. After the family had grown up, she returned to her Taoist studies. During her meditations she received many visits from the immortals who presented her with the first sections of the *Shang ch'ing* scriptures. When she died, her eldest son continued the teachings, and in particular involved an official called Yang Hsi.

In AD 364 Yang Hsi was summoned by spirits to Mount Mao, Kiangsu. Here he was visited by Wei Hua-ts'un. With her was a crowd of immortals and together they dictated to the astonished Yang Hsi the remainder of the scriptures. Over a fairly long period, Yang Hsi and two friends took down the revelations until a major collection had been given, to be added to those revealed to Wei Hua-ts'un herself during her life.

The collected scriptures filled a number of strong boxes, but their fate over the next hundred years or so was terrible. For reasons too complex to enter into here, the scriptures were sold off in pieces; stolen; given away as gifts; borrowed but rarely returned; copied and then forged; sold for sexual favours; plagiarised; sealed with molten lead; officially impounded and eventually re-collected, to the extent that this was possible, from all over China! Rarely, if ever, can sacred writings have been so abused before finding a final resting place within the first Canon of the Taoist Scriptures.

However, it would be a mistake to see the Mao Shan tradition's contribution as being solely scriptural. Alongside this tradition was that of the role of meditation in the search for truth and for immortality. The Mao Shan texts themselves present a vision of Taoist practices which sought for a less parochial, mundane or even ecstatic version than that offered by the two other main schools. They proposed peaceful meditation and reclusive lifestyle – in fact the sort of remote non-action (*wu-wei*) sage which so many associate with Taoism.

While these teachings are there in the *Shang ch'ing* scriptures, it was the example and teachings of one man who set the seal on the distinctive Mao Shan tradition. His name was T'ao Hung-ching, who lived himself on Mao Shan. Born in AD 456, he died in 536 and thus lived at that crucial point when the Taoist Canon was first written down. He helped to track down the original texts of the *Shang ch'ing* and published them for the elite world of his day. Ruling over a three-tiered centre, he held court for many of the most noble and wise people of his country. What he taught was very reminiscent of the more profound Buddhist meditational practices of his time, and as such he received many visits from Buddhist masters who spoke highly of him.

The heart of T'ao's teachings was that frankly much of the ritual and activities of the other Taoist schools was either so much hocus-pocus or, at the least, irrelevant. He taught that to achieve full awareness and possibly immortality, one needed to focus inwardly through pure meditation; empty the body and mind of all spirits and thoughts and thus prepare for union with the Ultimate Tao. Through this union, one could achieve immortality.

While T'ao taught the retreat and the reclusive Way of this meditation, his spiritual successor, Wang Yuan-chih (who reputedly was born in AD 525 and died in AD 655) took the teachings and made them accessible to a much wider population through the magnificent rituals and liturgies which he composed for cosmic union and renewal. This tradition continues today and is that which has most attracted outsiders to Taoism because of its beauty, simplicity and depth.

THE LING-PAO TRADITION

Finally we come to the *Ling-pao* tradition. This tradition also came into being during the fourth to sixth centuries but has no central teacher figure. Rather, it seems to have been almost a popularizing movement concerned with expressing through complex liturgies and rituals the teachings of the *Meng-wei* sect as well as drawing in other traditions. The title *Ling-pao* means 'Sacred Jewel' and refers to the sacred texts which lie at the centre of the sect. These texts were deemed to have been created when the Pure Breaths at the beginning of time fused and from their fusion came the tablets of the texts, jade tablets with gold lettering. These texts were preserved by the gods who then passed the teachings on to the Taoist adepts. The central book of the *Ling-pao* tradition is called the *Ling-pao wu-fu ching* – The Book of the Five Charms of the Sacred Jewel. Many of the rituals which the *Ling-pao* developed have passed into general use within Taoism to this day and whilst the tradition offered little of a 'profound' nature, they succeeded in making many of the core tenets of Taoism – magic, longevity and immortality – approachable at a popular level.

LATER CANONS

The net result of these three main schools working in their own individual ways, was that when in AD 471 the first Taoist Canon of Scripture was created, there were no less than twelve hundred scrolls in it. The next time a systematic Canon was recorded was in 748. The then Emperor, T'ang Hsuan-tsung (who believed himself to be a direct descendent of Lao Tzu) sent scholars and researchers out into the provinces of China to bring back the sacred texts. These were then compiled into the *Exquisite Compendium of the Three Canons* (the title is in itself an imitation of the Buddhist Tripitaka – the three baskets of the scriptures). The total of books or scrolls recorded in 748 was seven thousand three hundred! In 1019, the next revision of the Canon was made under directions from the Sung dynasty. The *Precious Canon of the Celestial Palace of the Great Sung* recorded a mere 4565 scrolls. Finally, in 1444 the most recent Canon was produced and printed, thus giving its selection wider authority. This was undertaken under the Ming ruler Ch'eng-tsu. Known as the *Scriptures of the Taoist Canon of the Great Ming*, it has fixed the Taoist Canon at 5318 scrolls, thus making it the largest Canon of Scripture in the world. Much of it is now completely incomprehensible as the language and symbolism is so obscure or else the last devotee of a particular scripture died hundreds of years ago and did not pass on the key of interpretation.

THE CH'UAN CH'EN SCHOOL

Last of all, in this examination of the main schools, we need to mention one other Taoist school which arose later than the three given above, but which has been as important, if not more so, than some of the original three. This is the *Ch'uan Ch'en* school, founded by Wang Chung-yang who lived in the twelfth century AD. It was an important school because it not only developed many of the aspects of monastic Taoism to a new level, but because it saw itself as drawing in the best of all three faiths then popular within China – Confucian, Buddhist and Taoist. Its collections of scriptures reflect this in that they contain the Lao Tzu and Shang-ch'ing classics of Taoism, the Confucian Canon of Filial Piety and the Buddhist text *Pan-juo Hsin-ching*. Its name, *Ch'uan Ch'en*, means 'Perfect Realization' but its secondary title is taken straight from Buddhism – the Golden Lotus Orthodox Religion (*Chin-lien Cheng-tsung*).

Legend has it that Wang Chung-yang was taught the new doctrines and practices by none other than the most famous of the Eight Immortals, Lu Tung Pin, of whom more later. The heart of the school was the retreat from the world of politics and worldly affairs. This involved not just retreating to some mountain fastness or into the exclusion of a strict monastery. It also included denying oneself the pleasures of the natural world, for to be attracted to anything was to succumb to satisfying the material needs and desires. Instead, the *Ch'uan Ch'en* Way was to enter into extreme states of meditation in order to suppress the yin tendency and elevate the yang. To do this, most members gave up all sleep and Wang himself spent two years ten feet down in the ground.

Even more remarkable were the developments pioneered under Wang's successor, the remarkable Ch'ang Ch'un. He saw Taoism as being the original truth, but felt that its purity and true meaning had become lost under a cloud of superstition and false teachings and practices. He rejected the search for chemical alchemy, instead turning inwards for transformation. He also rationalized the idea of the immortal, seeing this as meaning not some magical, eternal being, but rather as meaning a person who lived a good life and sought to be true to his principles.

It is perhaps worth mentioning here a very common type of Taoist. He was rarely, if ever, attached to one of the main schools, for he was a wanderer. Using skills and tricks learnt on the road or picked up in temples and monasteries, the wandering Taoists were a common feature of Chinese society and literature. Often charlatans, they nevertheless served many people in remote areas in ways that the more regular Taoists could not.

Taoist Abbot

We have not looked at Taoist monasticism in any detail. It differed little from what we would expect of such communities, except that the monasteries were often quite remote and rather lax. Taoist monks did not have a good reputation for holiness, though of course, where a master teacher lived, a worthy community would often gather.

It is now time to turn and look seriously at that quest which has been mentioned throughout this book, the quest for immortality.

6 · THE QUEST FOR IMMORTALITY

It is probably true to say that in no country other than China have so many people poisoned themselves into an early grave in the search for long life and immortality! Just as cigarette packets now bear health warnings, so should the old manuals of Taoism on bodily immortality.

It is not often appreciated by the West that the Chinese idea of immortality was primarily that of the eternity of both the spirit or soul and the body. Without the body, there could be no immortality. Thus the quest was not just for meditational release from the constraints of life and death, but for transformation of the physical body into an eternal vehicle for the spirit. This is why Taoist immortality involves not just meditation and development of the spirit but also the hunt for the magical pill, elixir or method which would ensure that the body would be transformed into an everlasting human frame capable of bearing the spirit and of being united to the One Origin and to Heaven and Earth for ever.

As we saw earlier, the desire for immortality was already active amongst the ancient rulers of China from at least the fifth century BC. Ssu-ma Ch'ien mentions a number of them specifically from the fourth century BC onwards. Before that, it is hard to tell. Some scholars believe that there was always a cult of longevity and certainly it was a feature of all the most ancient rulers, such as the Three August Ones or the Five August Emperors, that they lived for a long time. It also seems to have been a theme within these legends that this ability to live for two or three hundred years was progressively lost as one came nearer and nearer to historical times. In other words, it was a feature of the Chinese Golden Age and in these less pure, less worthy times, this gift has been diminished and all but lost. Certainly, these most ancient heroes do not, in the earliest accounts, achieve immortality. They live a long time, die and are then in many cases deified. However, as this was a process which could be undertaken by descendants – they communicated with Heaven and announced that their worthy ancestor was now a god – this does not betoken any idea of immortality as such. Other scholars feel that in the shamanist's vision of the interaction between the spirit world and the material world, one finds the idea of the person who not only communicates between these two worlds, but is actually able to pass from one to the other, from the material to the spiritual. However, the evidence for this is much thinner.

So we really have no idea where these ideas came from. What is interesting is that while some Chinese today will still tell you that it is possible to become an immortal, most will not, but will tell you about how to extend your life. Even at the height of the Cultural Revolution, the Chinese newspapers carried reports of people who through self-discipline, a healthy diet or because of the regenerative powers of the words of Marx, Lenin and Mao Tse-tung, had been able to live well into their second century. Any Chinese festival, celebration or greeting of best wishes will invariably contain the wish for long life. It is one of the basic tenets of what a good life is – namely that you live long, have lots of children, grow wealthy and be of a comfortable girth! While immortality may be the more fascinating theologically and historically, it is longevity which has retained its place in the hearts of the ordinary Chinese. I think it is important to bear this in mind, otherwise you can come away from some books on Taoism and immortality convinced that the whole of China was involved in alchemy or strange practices in the quest for immortality. For most Chinese, the salvationary, healing and exorcism faith of Taoism, mixed with Buddhism and ancestor worship, provided sufficent answers to life's existential questions.

APPROACHES TO IMMORTALITY

We have already looked at the first Emperor's search for the Isles of the Blessed and for the magic elixir. As Ssu-ma Ch'ien noted, all the emperors seem to have been interested in this quest. Indeed, there is a lovely story of one such emperor, which is told at the time of the Mid-Autumn Festival. On this day the harvest moon is the brightest of the year. The Chinese believe that they can see a young woman, a rabbit and a tree on the moon. How did the young woman come to be there? Well, she was the wife of a cruel and vicious emperor who oppressed his people and abused his power. He had sent Taoists all over the world to find the pill of immortality. To the considerable consternation of his people – and his long-suffering wife – the pill was found and brought to the palace.

The emperor declared that he would devour the pill the next day and thus become immortal. The people were not happy at the idea of this unpleasant man ruling them into eternity. Nor was the wife happy. So, that night, she crept into the room where the pill lay. Picking it up she was just wondering what to do with it, when in burst the emperor. Furious, he rushed towards her meaning to kill her. Not knowing what to do, she swallowed the pill so that he should not have it. Instantly she found herself floating up from the ground, well beyond the desperate reaches of her husband. In no time at all, she had floated to the moon where the gods placed her to protect her. Great was the rejoicing on earth when it was discovered that the emperor had been robbed of his planned immortality, and each year the festival celebrates the brave young woman and she smiles down on the earth – which is why the moon is so bright that night.

This story captures perfectly one of the main points about the quest for immortality. It was not a quest which the ordinary people could follow. It called for immense wealth, if you were to follow the alchemist's route, or immense patience and no need to work, if you were to follow the sage's path of meditation and discipline. For ninety-nine per cent of the people, this was impossible. However, the immortals were very important because they featured as the great heroes and heroines of Chinese literature, especially folk literature. In their lives and exploits the Chinese lived out their greatest hopes and dreams. This is a dimension of the immortals which often gets overlooked by western writers who concentrate on the practices rather than on the symbolic role of these beings. So let us try and fuse the two by looking through the stories as well as at the historical developments in order to understand better the significance of the immortals and the quest for immortality.

Putting it crudely, there were two approaches to immortality. One required external potions, pills, elixirs and suchlike, often requiring alchemy; the other was concerned with internal transformation through control of the natural body and meditation. There is great debate as to which is the earliest and which is, therefore, the purest tradition. I do not believe that we can find evidence of either practice in the *Tao Te Ching*. Chuang Tzu certainly refers to certain practices, but in such mocking terms as to make us doubt that he saw them as a serious tradition. These descriptions, as I have argued in the section on Chuang Tzu, do not relate to the idea of the Perfect Man. The Perfect Man is an ideal, not a goal.

What is certain is that when the quest first appears in the historical records, it is concerned almost exclusively with the external model. Hence the search for the Isles of the Blessed where the pill can be found, or the quest for magical herbs and the like. Whatever the early emperors were interested in, it was not sitting and meditating – at least, not for long! It is only in Chuang Tzu's references to such figures as the Yellow Emperor that we hear of such meditational practices unifying the individual with the eternal Tao and thus achieving immortality. But this is aetiological and, as we have seen, is simply an explanation for his divine status, not a universally applicable formula.

What is derived from the early Taoist classics, and, as I have argued earlier, from certain key ideas in shamanism, is the notion that Humanity is one of three pillars of existence. There is Heaven and Earth, and then there is the sage/ruler who represents Humanity. These three forces control the ebb and flow of life. The most crucial role is that of the ruler who seeks to ensure that the world is run along the lines of the Tao – the Natural Way. The argument was then developed that of these three pillars of existence, only the human is perishable. The other two are eternal in their given forms. The assumption was made that at one stage we humans must also have been eternal but that this attribute was lost. This then found expression in the two schools of thought about how to achieve immortality. The first sought to try to make the human body an imperishable form;

94

the second sought to seek such union with the Tao through internal focus and meditation, that the material became Tao and thus eternal, for the Tao cannot die. It was the philosophical schools which began the development of the latter, bringing its ideas into the mixture which produced Taoism, whilst the concept of material transformation was developed in a much more piecemeal fashion, continuing well into the early Christian era.

THE IMPERISHABLE BODY

Let us start then with the quest for the imperishable body. The logic was quite simple. The world contained materials which were imperishable such as gold, jade or mercury. If the fleshly body could be transformed or replaced progressively by such imperishable materials, then immortality would ensue. Thus it was that those seeking immortality were fed on ground up jade, flakes of gold, or more lethally, mercury. The idea was that by introducing small quantities into the diet of the person, the body would absorb the imperishable materials and transformation would gradually be achieved. Needless to say, nothing of the sort happened, and a lot of people died in great agony and pain from metal poisoning. Certainly, as Joseph Needham (in his volumes on *Science and Civilisation in China*) has clearly illustrated, the experiments on the materials which preceded these diets led the Chinese into making some very fundamental early scientific discoveries. However, it also failed to achieve what it really wanted and caused illness and death instead – but I suppose much scientific research has had that sort of effect!

A gentler way to find immortality was the search for herbs and prescriptions which could achieve the desired transformation in a more magical way. Mushrooms were greatly favoured, as were vital parts of animals which were believed to live for a very long time. Cranes, turtles, tortoises, cicadas, bats and butterflies were particularly esteemed and were thus to be found cooking gently in the pots of the shamans and Taoists searching for immortality. Having said that, there has always been a strong vegetarian tradition in Taoism, albeit a minority movement.

95

ALCHEMY

Alongside this quest for immortality ran the quest for the formula to create gold. The fact that both such enterprises were funded by the emperors should come as no surprise. The desire to rule for ever is not a twentieth century quirk! And, as ever, rulers were short of cash to maintain their troops, palaces and lifestyle. Thus the two seem to have been undertaken together from at least the second century BC.

Despite the total failure to succeed, the quest continued. Perhaps the comment of the Han dynasty Emperor Wu (141–87 BC) is typical. It is also rather touching. Wu spent vast amounts of money on ships to search for the Blessed Isles; on magic formulas and on alchemy, but all to no avail. At the end of his life he commented:

'If we are temperate in our diet and use medicine, we make our illnesses few. That is all we can attain to.'

But still the quest went on, until a major failure pulled the plug on official sponsorship for many years.

THE MASTER OF THE FORMULAS

The Emperor Han Hsuan Ti (73–48 BC) was as keen as anyone for immortality. Within his own family he had a cousin who had already gained some notoriety as a Taoist/fang-shih. In the year 60 BC, this cousin, Liu Hsiang, came before his revered relative the Emperor and claimed that, if granted enough financial resources, he could produce gold, and thus also the elixir of life. When questioned as to how, Liu Hsiang replied that he had obtained various books which would show him the way. The Emperor duly appointed him and gave him the title of the Master of the Formulas.

For four years, at great expense, and with a considerable amount of public fanfare, Liu Hsiang sought to understand the books and to achieve success, but it eluded him year after year. At last, in 56 BC, the Emperor's patience and money ran out and he ordered that Liu Hsiang be executed. This would surely have happened had not Liu's brother persuaded the Emperor to let him off with a massive fine. Liu Hsiang's comment on the whole affair was that he had failed because although he had the books, he had no master to interpret them for him. The comment of the rest of Chinese society was one of considerable scepticism which put the lid on any further 'serious' work in this area for a long time.

It is not until the middle of the second century AD that we find alchemy publicly raising its head again. Obviously it had continued throughout this time, but not in an overtly public way. The first book on alchemy of which we are aware was published around AD 140. The author is Wei Po-yang and the book is virtually unintelligible. It is a series of cryptic formulas designed to help achieve immortality. Its main ingredient is cinnabar, or mercury sulphide which, being blood red in hue, was considered to be very auspicious. In this difficult book, Wei explains that its purpose is to help people understand the process of alchemy and that he wrote it because he was upset about the many people who had bankrupted themselves trying to follow difficult formulas! We can take it that by the middle of the second century AD, all the major features of alchemy as a doorway to immortality were well in place.

KO HUNG

The most significant figure in the establishing of the alchemy tradition of Taoism, as well as being linked to the internal school, was a remarkable gentleman by the name of Ko Hung. Born around AD 250, he lived to be 81 and during his life compiled a vast study of Taoist practices called the *Pao P'u Tzu*, which Needham translates as The Book of the Preservation-of-Solidarity Master. This tome is a guide to all the known ways of becoming an immortal. As such it draws material from many different schools and makes for a fascinating read. It contains material which contradicts other sections, material which even Ko cannot explain and material which is amusing. Its centre, however, is alchemical, for while Ko Hung believed you could become a sort of immortal without alchemy, he did not believe eternity could be fully achieved without such practices. In the writings of Ko Hung we see alchemy reach its highest point, for after that it seems to have become less popular, taking second place after the internal school. This shift is also to be observed in Ko Hung's tome where he says:

'Those who do not carry out acts of virtue and are satisfied only to practise magical procedures will never obtain life eternal.'

97

So let us turn back to see what the other path offered – apart from a sounder diet!

INTERNAL TRANSFORMATION

The second path was the one of inner purification and union with the Tao. While this used quasi-medical preparations, the heart of this practice was meditation and inner reflection upon the forces inherent within the body and their unity with the Ultimate, the One Origin, the Tao.

Essentially, the body was seen as being given life and sustained by two forces. The first and most important was energy which expressed itself particularly in the breath. This energy, known as ch'i, was what made life possible for the body. The Taoists identified many different kinds of breaths which circulated through the body, not all of them benevolent. It was therefore important to try to preserve and sustain those which were beneficial whilst ridding oneself of the malevolent. Particular attention was paid to the Embryonic Breath. This was the original breath which had entered the body in the womb. There was great fascination in trying to discover where and how the original, Embryonic Breath actually entered the foetus. It was felt that if this original breath could be found and preserved then immortality would ensue. Thus an array of practices were developed to ensure that the air in the body was retained and sustained. This led to the development of breathing exercises designed to prolong the retention of air, for in the act of breathing out one surely lost some of the vital breath which ensured life. And attention was not paid just to the mouth and nose. Air, as we all know to our cost, can escape from another part of the body! This is why diet was also important and why items such as the onion and certain kinds of grain and beans were forbidden.

SEXUAL PRACTICES

The other life-giving and sustaining force is semen. It needs to be stated here that whilst there were indeed famous Taoist women, and even in the Eight Immortals there is a woman, women did not feature highly in Taoism. Taoism was and is no different from all other main religions in being primarily patriarchal. Thus women were simply not considered to be as important as men. After all, of the Eight Immortals, only one was a woman.

Semen regarded as a life-giving force was an obvious deduction. What the students of this school sought to do was to ensure that this life-giving force was not wasted, for in doing so, part of the life force was spent. Rather they tried to develop techniques whereby the semen arose but was not expelled from the body but was recycled within the body. This involved a variety of practices such as sexual intercourse until immediately before ejaculation, whereupon the man would then squeeze his penis in such a way as to drive the semen back into his own body to sustain and rebuild it. The height of achievement was when the semen was fused with the Embryonic Breath and together they formed a new embryo which then dwelt within the old body of the man, growing slowly, ready to issue forth as an immortal body when the old body died.

There are plenty of copiously illustrated books which explore the use of intercourse and sexual positions in this quest for immortality. What does need saying is that whilst sexual practices were common within the family relationship of husband and wife, or husband, wife and his concubines, there was also an orgiastic dimension which flourished for a while but has achieved a notoriety far beyond its actual worth. It does seem that during the T'ang dynasty in particular, mass sexual festivals or events took place. These were carried out in secret, for even then they were considered unworthy of the Tao, or rather unworthy of Chinese culture. Along with these rituals there was also a considerable literature on sex and the Way which was included in the T'ang and Sung Canons of the scriptures but was omitted by the time of the final Ming edition in AD 1444.

In essence, much of the sexual practice was a form of the exercises described below combined with the production and retention of semen. It was not encouraged by any of the major schools, especially not for those who were monks. But it was a perfectly legitimate development for interested laymen and as such should be understood within the wider physiognomical and psychological framework of the quest for immortality.

PHYSICAL EXERCISES

The body was also perceived as a battlefield. In traditional Chinese anatomy, the body was a microcosm of the universe. That is to say, it contained the opposites of yin and yang; it contained a vast array of internal gods; it contained the vital breaths but also three worms whose job was to destroy the body and its ch'i. Thus the Taoist following these teachings sought to balance the yin and yang; to sustain and respect the gods in the different parts of his body and to overcome the attempts by the three worms to stifle and destroy the vital forces of ch'i within the body. To do this required patience and peace. A vast array of exercises was developed to enable the body to be relaxed and in balance; to be able to flex and thus enliven all parts of the body; to sooth taut parts of the body where the worms were in action. These beautiful and extremely beneficial exercises are one of the most persistent and visible forms of Taoist influence on Chinese culture today. Go to any park in China or Chinese areas of the world and you will find people undertaking these exercises. While no one in their right minds would give a moment's thought to the swallowing of mercury or gold today, many in both East and West have found the Taoist exercises for immortality helpful in coping with the pressures of modern day life.

The peace and quiet needed to carry out these exercises over many years led Taoists to retreat into the mountains and other quiet places. Indeed the very word for an immortal in Chinese is made up of two other characters meaning man and mountain. It was, therefore, synonymous with a rejection of the official life and values of China. This is beautifully captured in the story of how Lu Tung Pin became one of the Eight Immortals.

Lu Tung Pin was a well placed and popular official with a bright future in front of him. One day he was travelling between one city and another when he came at midday to a little wayside inn. Unbeknown to him, the immortal Han Chung Li was sitting at a table there. Lu Tung Pin sat down beside him and the two soon fell to talking and drinking together. Han Chung Li could see that this man was of far higher quality than the usual official. The day was cold, the wine was warm and the fire was roaring well. Thus it was not long before Lu Tung Pin fell asleep. As he slept, he had a most convincing dream. He dreamt that he rose swiftly through the ranks of the officials, achieving higher and yet higher positions until at last he became the prime minister. For twenty years he and his family enjoyed all the fruits of his high position and the trust of the Emperor. What more could mortal man require, he thought. But then disaster struck. He offended the Emperor and fell from favour. Immediately his enemies closed in and began to whisper to the Emperor that Lu Tung Pin was out to depose him. In great anger the Emperor had all of Lu Tung Pin's family executed before his very eyes and then banished him to a far away land.

It was at this point that Lu Tung Pin awoke to find himself covered in sweat, but still seated beside Han Chung Li. Immediately Lu Tung Pin realised that he was in the presence of an immortal and he also realized the futility of an official's life. Giving it all up, he went off into the mountains seeking the True Way. For many years he studied under Han Chung Li until he too achieved immortality.

THE MORAL DIMENSION

In later years the quest for immortality developed a more moral dimension as well. That is to say, in imitation of the Buddhist concept of merit leading to salvation, the Taoists introduced the idea of the achievement of immortality as a reward from the gods for particularly worthy acts. The following story illustrates this development.

A copy of a renowned Taoist book had been handed down from generation to generation within one family. Eventually it became the property of Wan Tei Hsu who cared for it and honoured it greatly. One day a Taoist priest came to visit the family. Wan asked him to talk to them about the Tao.

'The soul is Tao,' said the priest, 'and the Tao is soul. The soul and Tao are not different in essence. If the Tao is separated from the soul, you will suffer rebirth in all of the six major realms as well as be bound by the three paths (of lust, greed and anger). But if the soul and the Tao are united, then you will reach paradise and the land of the immortals. Hell and Heaven are in your own heart. Unless Heaven resides in you, simply reading the sacred texts will give you nothing.'

He then turned to Wan and said that the house contained a rare jewel, for its radiance had struck him as he entered. So doing he indicated the sacred book. He advised Wan and his family that this book contained all the wisdom that was needed to achieve immortality. If they followed the book's teachings, they would be saved and brought to the realm of the immortals.

For thirty years Wan did exactly that. He gave to those in need and sought to improve the lives of all around him. One day, his neighbours heard divine music and rushing out of their homes they were in time to see the entire Wan family being transported to Heaven as immortals.

This story is one of the many improving tales in the *T'ai Shang Kan Ying P'ien*, and, of course, this is the very book so venerated by the family. It is none other than the second book which Taoism ascribes to Lao Tzu. The book, which is far more popular in China than the *Tao Te Ching* – indeed was the most printed book in imperial China – is called the *T'ai Shang Kan Ying P'ien*. This means the Writings of the Highest One on Response and Retribution. The Highest One is, of course, Lao Tzu in his divine form. The book claims to have been written around the time of the *Tao Te Ching*. It is, in fact, clearly of the late Sung period. However, it has been revered in China as being written by Lao Tzu and in one sense it is a sort of pot-boiler version of Taoism for the lay person. It is full of worthy sentiments and instructions about how to live a decent life in accordance with Taoist principles. It also clearly shows that it is possible to earn your way to immortality. In pre-Revolutionary China, simply to pay for the printing and distribution of this book was taken to be an act of great merit which could assist you on the path to immortality or at the least, to wealth and longevity.

THE EIGHT IMMORTALS

Before we leave the theme of immortality, it is important to look in a little more detail at the Eight Immortals. As I have said, the quest for immortality, either through the alchemical route or the internal/introspective route, was the pursuit of the few, although an object of fascination to the many. As such, for the majority of people, Taoist and others, the immortals were important for other reasons. There was little expectation of achieving immortality, not even through virtuous acts, but there was a widespread belief that sincere people could be helped to survive in their everyday life by the intervention of the immortals. This was and is especially true of the Eight Immortals who are worshipped and invoked daily around the world by the Chinese to this day. Not only are they venerated for answering prayers or sorting out difficulties, but they also fight against oppression and injustice. They are, in fact, a combination between Robin Hood and Superman and as such are vastly popular! The eight represent a cross-section of the lower to middle ranges of Chinese society.

102

LU TUNG PIN

Lu Tung Pin, of whose conversion experience we have already heard, is strongly associated with the alchemical tradition and with the elixir of life. It was from Lu Tung Pin that Wang Chung-yang, the founder of the *Ch'uan Ch'en* school, claimed to have received his teachings. In temples today, people with illnesses will go and ask advice from Lu Tung Pin and medicinal formulas with his name attached are given great standing. Lu Tung Pin is also associated with charms and powers over demons. Like Chang Tao Ling, he wields a mighty demon sword with which he keeps the evil forces at bay. These twin roles of medicine and charms often overlap.

TI KUAI LI

Ti Kuai Li, along with Lu, is the most popular of the immortals. Although he is an immortal, he is also a hideously deformed cripple. But he was not always so. As a mortal Ti Kuai Li was a handsome man who took himself off into the hills to study immortality. After many years he had learnt to ride the clouds and could undertake journeys of astral travel. When he did so he always left one of his disciples in charge of his body to ensure that nothing happened to it. One day Ti announced that he was off to visit Lao Tzu. He told his disciple to guard his body, but if he had not returned to it by the end of the seventh day, he was to destroy it because he would be dead.

The student faithfully sat beside the body. However, on the sixth day, a messenger came from his mother. She was dying and longed to see him. The student was desperate. Whom should he serve – his master or his mother? In the end the student decided that his master, gone for six days, must be dead. So he burnt the body and went on his way to see his mother.

A few hours later Ti Kuai Li returned. He wandered up and down the road looking for his body. Then he came upon the pile of ashes and realized that it was gone! He now had a very short period of time in which to find a new body within which to dwell. If he did not find one quickly – and it would have to be a very newly dead body – then he would simply die. In the distance he spotted such a body. Rushing over, he saw to his horror and disgust that it was the body of an old, crippled beggar. However, there was no time to lose, so into the body he went. And it is in this form that he now dwells forever!

As you can imagine, this means he is <u>not</u> always in the best of moods! So he is not much use to pray to, though he is favoured by doctors. The reason for his popularity is that he fights for the weak, helpless and oppressed, as you will hear later.

CHANG KUO LAU

Next comes Chang Kuo Lau. He is another strange figure, often shown riding a donkey backwards. He is especially favoured by couples seeking offspring for he is believed to bring fertility and especially baby boys. The reason for his riding backwards is rather interesting. Chang Kuo Lau came from a poor but hard-working farmer's family. It was Kuo Lau's job to take the produce to market, which he did riding a donkey. One day he stopped off at a deserted temple to rest. Waking from his sleep, he smelt a wonderful smell. Searching all over the temple, he eventually found a pot full of strange herbs cooking gently. It looked so good he ate it. In doing so he had great good fortune, for it was in fact the brew of a skilled alchemist who had found the recipe for immortality. Unwittingly, Chang had become immortal. But no sooner had he eaten his fill and given a little to his donkey, than the alchemist ran up. Seeing Chang, he shouted at him. In panic, Chang leapt backwards onto the donkey, and the donkey, similarly alarmed, raced off. In a few moments, the pair of them were flying through the air, immortals both, and neither Chang nor the donkey ever looked back, so to speak!

So here is an immortal who becomes one through being a good lad but also through good luck. Luck such as this is an important factor in the popularity of the Eight Immortals. After all, we could all have the luck of Chang – maybe.

TS'AO KUO CHIU

Ts'ao Kuo Chiu is the one aristocrat in the entire bunch. He is a very strange person, having been a murderer who repented of his ways, but only because he had no option. Quite why he is included in the Eight is a mystery.

HAN HSIANG TZU

Han Hsiang Tzu is a different kettle of fish. He is a musician and carries his flute. He is usually depicted on the mountains, listening to the music of nature. Han Hsiang Tzu is a true Taoist mountain sage.

HAN CHUNG LI

We know enough about Han Chung Li to be able to assert that he was a real person. He was a general in the later Han dynasty. He is associated with alchemy for he carries the peach of immortality which, if devoured, will ensure immortality to the eater. This has echoes of the oldest traditions, such as the Isles of the Blessed, where such fruit could be found.

LAN TS'AI HO

Lan Ts'ai Ho is apparently a transvestite. He appears sometimes as a woman, sometimes as a man. As such he represents the outcast, the lunatic, the one 'touched by God' in the Eight.

HO HSIEN KU

Finally we come to the one woman in the group, Ho Hsien Ku. She was made an immortal because of both her generosity and her severe asceticism.

THE POPULARITY OF THE EIGHT IMMORTALS

In these types we can see the range of paths to immortality – including some which are not often discussed, such as cheeky good luck. While they are important in helping us put the great theories of immortality into some perspective, the chief function of the Eight Immortals is as fighters for the underdog, namely the vast majority of the Chinese down through history. Let one tale suffice to give you an idea of why the Eight Immortals were, and continue to be, so popular.

The Eight Immortals liked to meet at the Immortals' Bridge to drink and chat. One day, Chang Kuo Lau called for silence. Then he told them a scandalous story. Far away in a distant province there was a wealthy man called K'uang Tzu Lien. He would soon be sixty, which is a great time of celebration in China. To honour this day he had invited his friends to a vast feast. However, his wealth came from the sweat of his poor labourers who were to be given nothing. Worse than that, he was so rich and contemptuous of the poor, he had ordered them to fill in the pot holes on the road to his estate with rice and then cover it with rich red wool for his guests to travel on.

The Eight sat in stunned amazement. Then Ti Kuai Li leapt to his feet. 'How dare he waste rice which could feed the poor and squander cloth which could clothe them. He needs to be taught a lesson.'

So saying, Ti leapt off and, travelling upon the clouds, he soon reached K'uang's house. There he took on the full appearance of a beggar, complete with begging bowl. Hundreds of beggars were near the house which was strongly guarded. Ti went straight up to five of the guards and asked for some food. Laughing, the guards hit him about the head until he fell down. Trying to get up, Ti grasped a handful of rice from under the red carpet, but seeing this the guards kicked him.

'Please let me take some of this rice to feed my starving children,' begged Ti, to which the guards replied that their master would rather it was crushed to dust than be given to beggars who spoiled his party. Then Ti said in a deep and threatening voice, 'The rich should beware of cheating the needy and insulting the poor.' Enraged, the guards beat Ti even harder and then stormed off. The other beggars rushed to help Ti up and warned him to stay away. But Ti vowed vengeance.

Inside the house, a vast feast was ready and hundreds of rich guests seated. The first course was brought in. At first all was well, but then the bowls became red hot and the guests had great difficulty eating from them. Suddenly one gave a scream, followed by another and another. The food in their bowls had turned rotten and was full of maggots. The servants rushed around clearing the food away and bringing in the next course. But no sooner had this touched the table than it too turned rotten.

K'uang was furious but guessed that it was the fault of the impudent beggar. He ordered him to be brought before him. Bleeding from head and body, Ti stood before K'uang and told

106

him he was just a simple beggar. Then, dramatically Ti dropped dead. K'uang ordered his guards to fling the body out and for the feast to continue. But the other beggars had seen all this and ran to the local magistrate who was renowned for his honesty. The magistrate set out straight away. When he arrived, he found K'uang and his guests in a terrible state. They had been unable to move Ti's body.

The magistrate realized that something strange was going on. He called a Taoist priest from the crowd and asked him to examine the body. On a slip of paper in Ti's pocket were found the following words: 'I do not want K'uang to pay for this crime with his life. I want him to sweep the roads leading from his house to all the towns and villages of this province. He must learn that a rich man cannot cheat the poor.'

Suddenly the magistrate realised that Ti was none other than one of the Eight Immortals. K'uang was arrested and all his goods were confiscated and shared out among the poor. From that day on he swept the roads of the province. And Ti? Well, the good people put him, now light as a feather, inside a coffin. Because of legal difficulties they had to wait some days before his funeral could take place. When they came to lift the coffin, it was so light they were alarmed. Prising off the lid they found only Ti's clothes inside. Ti himself had returned to the other immortals drinking and eating at the Immortals' Bridge, long before.

POETS AND SAGES

Finally, in our study of immortality and of the different streams which have flowed in and out of the river of Taoism, let us look at the poets, the philosophers and the humorists who, in their own idiosyncratic and often sarcastic way, followed the Tao and left their mark on Chinese culture. For in their actions and especially in their writings, they have indeed achieved immortality.

THE SEVEN SAGES

One of my children's favourite stories is of Liu Ling. He lived from AD 220 to 300 and was one of the famous, or infamous, Seven Sages of the Bamboo Grove, a bunch of drunken Taoist poets. They were notorious for their non-action and passivity which scandalized their Confucian contemporaries. The story my children so love is of Liu Ling at home. He was prone to walking around his house naked which was not quite the done thing. One day a group of rather pompous Confucians came to complain of his general behaviour. They were ushered into his study only to find Liu Ling stark naked. Horrified, they expressed their distress at being confronted by him without his trousers on. Liu Ling looked astonished. 'But the whole universe is my city; the world is my local area; my city is my home; and my rooms are my clothes. What are you lot doing in my trousers?'

It is hard to know quite what to make of the Seven Sages or others of that time who belonged to the Pure Conversation school. At times I think they were simply taking the micky out of all conventions, rather like a more cynical and wicked Chuang Tzu. For instance, some claimed that Confucius was a better Taoist than Lao Tzu or Chuang Tzu. Why? Because they only talked about non-action – K'ung actually achieved it. When it was pointed out to them that K'ung never talks about this, they answered that this just showed how far advanced he was in that he never even took the action to tell others about it!

The Seven Sages represent another dimension. They simply laughed at every convention and became adepts of the theory of *feng liu* – departing from convention – such as Liu Ling and his trousers. The key figure of the group was Hsi K'ang, a wealthy man who lived close to an area known as the Bamboo Grove. Here the friends would meet to drink and talk and write poetry. In seeking to escape the conditioning and restraints of convention, they were looking for both the genuineness of experience and the path to immortality. It would appear that many of them were engaged also in internal school exercises for immortality and a few dabbled in alchemy of a rather medicinal nature. But it is the freeness of their prose and the liveliness of their affirmation of life which is so touching. Take, for instance, this opening verse from Liu Ling's Hymn to the Virtue of Wine. It uses many terms which are familiar to those who know their *Tao Te Ching* or their *Chuang Tzu*, but in a context which would have surprised the one and probably surprised but also amused the other.

'He is a noble master,
For whom Heaven and Earth are but a morning,
And eternity but an instant;
Sun and moon are his windows;
The eight deserts are his court;
He walks without leaving traces;
He dwells in no house;
For the roof he has heaven and for mat earth,
He follows his fancy.'
(translated by Henri Maspero in *Taoism and Chinese Religion*.)

Many scholars regard the Seven Sages and others in this period of the third to fourth centuries AD as being in some way a return or renaissance of the true, philosophical Taoism. As I have argued earlier, this never really existed as a self-conscious school anyway and whatever the Seven Sages and friends were, they were not latter-day Lao Tzus. Instead they seem to be an anti-establishment movement which arose at a time of dynastic disintegration. They come only just after the Yellow Turban Rebellion – another response to collapsing structures and authority. But instead of taking the path of resistance in the name of a greater Unity, they took the path of non-action. In their advocacy of this non-action and of spontaneity, they certainly took one strand of Taoist thinking to its logical conclusion, but it is over-romanticizing them to claim that they are the true heirs to 'philosophical Taoism', as well as being a far too serious response to what were, in fact, a fascinating group of rebels against everything – including much of philosophical Taoism.

As I hinted at the beginning, this group achieved far greater immortality than most of those we have named in the various other schools of immortality because they wrote personal poetry about the human condition which has continued to speak to the Chinese over the centuries and now reaches a wider audience.

The movement was short-lived. Hsi K'ang was, in fact, executed in AD 262 because he got caught up in a nasty adultery case. He refused to have anything to do with the courts and the particular case and so out of spite he was imprisoned and executed. It seemed that even the path of non-action and departure from convention could not break free of some of the harsher realities of an empire in decline, and the movement, if it ever was as grand as that, faded away, leaving its prose and poetry as its memorial.

7 · VISITING THE EARTH GOD
RENEWING THE COSMOS

So what of Taoism today? In recent years the West has been flooded
by many books which claim to reveal Taoism to the uninitiated.
Much of this has been rubbish of the most extraordinary sort. The
most bizarre and ridiculous theories, personal idiosyncrasies and
cultural angsts have been hung on Taoism, and in the process it
has become even more obscure and unfathomable than before. Thus
when Westerners go to China or the Far East looking for this sort of
Taoism, they do not find it, for it does not exist. What they will find
is a living faith which has suffered more dramatically in the last forty
years under Communism than at any time in its history. They will
find that in Chinese cities which once had seventy or eighty Taoist
temples, there will now be only two or three left. They will find
that the great Taoist holy mountains are still visited by hundreds,
even thousands of pilgrims who make their way painfully up to the
summit on their knees. But alongside them will be tens of thousands
of tourists out for the day. They will still find a few reclusive monks
preparing for immortality, mostly through meditational means. They
can visit a handful of Taoist temples where little seems to be
happening and only a few monks continue the age old traditions.

110

Yet, for all this, Taoism is still very much alive and living within Chinese culture. In many areas, the old Taoist 'parish' priest is returning to perform rites of passage, exorcise ghosts and perform other rituals. The Communist authorities increasingly complain about the growth in numbers of wandering Taoist monks who travel from place to place offering, what are at times, their rather dubious wares and skills. But it is in the family life and everyday life of the Chinese that we can find Taoist beliefs and practices alive and well.

Traditional funeral with Taoist priest

TAOISM TODAY

Take an average family in Hong Kong. In the morning, probably before they have breakfast, the family or a member of it will make an offering to the earth god of the house or flat. This will often simply be some joss sticks offered with a prayer, though tea and cakes are sometimes proffered. The earth god is a totally Taoist deity. He or she represents the primal force or deity (often represented as five deities) who inhabit that place. Any activity which is planned has to receive the permission of the earth god. The earth god is responsible for the

111

well-being of his or her locality to the district god. The district god is responsible to the city god, who is responsible to the county god – and so on. The Taoist pantheon reflects exactly imperial authority as it descended down through the ranks of officials as we shall see later.

After worshipping the earth god, the family may well make an offering to the ancestors. While ancestor worship pre-dates Taoism, much of the ritual is derived from Taoist rituals. On their way out of the home, the family members may well check with the almanac to see what sort of day it will be and which are the most auspicious hours. The almanac, hanging by its red cord beside the main door, is not just a vast repository of Taoist beliefs, charms and divination systems, but is also a charm in its own right. If any member of the family is making a major journey, or starting a new venture on a certain day, then the date will have been chosen with reference to the almanac, the T'ung Shu. No major decision is taken without consulting the almanac.

The home itself and any place of business will have been surveyed by a feng shui master. The art of feng shui, which literally translated means wind/water, is the system by which the forces dwelling in and controlling the land and environment are related to the horoscopes of the individuals living there. Feng shui affects not just what is built but also where. It seeks to combat evil influences and adverse forces by the use of powerful Taoist charms and rituals.

Leaving the home and travelling to work, the family will almost certainly see people practising t'ai-chi-ch'uan. This meditative exercising of the body will be taking place on any open space, be that a park or the end of the station platform. The purpose of t'ai-chi-ch'uan is to ensure the flow of the vital energy force – ch'i – throughout the body, thus maintaining the essential balances and harmonies within the body. These ideas are rooted in Taoist beliefs and practices, for t'ai-chi-ch'uan was developed in the remote monasteries of Taoism.

If someone is ill in the family, then most families will resort to a mixture of traditional Chinese medicine and western medicine. In using traditional medicine they are locking into a set of beliefs about how the various forces within the body must be balanced and about the body per se. These beliefs spring directly from Taoism. For instance, Taoism teaches that the body is a microcosm of the universe and that within us are thousands of deities which mirror

112

exactly the celestial order. Indeed, so close is the link between Taoism and traditional medicine that Buddhist monks, anxious to stress and keep their distinct identity, were forbidden to practise medicine.

Let us assume that our family has, despite the *feng shui*, been troubled by a ghost, a not uncommon experience in Chinese society. To deal with it they will probably call upon the local Taoist priest. A true Taoist master will know just from the description of the ghost's activities what sort of spirit it is and thus what to do about it and what charm to use.

At most of the major festivals Taoist charms, rituals and prayers will be used. At New Year, for instance, the kitchen god is worshipped. This deity sits in the kitchen and watches over the intimate goings on of the family. Just before New Year the paper image of the god or dedicatory inscription is burnt in order to send the god to Heaven.

Just in this brief journey around the Chinese family we can see how Taoist ideas and beliefs shape and give meaning to their lives. Put alongside this the role of fortune-telling and divination which is often linked directly to a Taoist deity, such as Wong Tai Sin, and the place which the tales and legends of the Taoists have in popular culture, and you can see that Taoism is an essential part of Chinese culture.

Looking at Taoism today, there are three main ways in which the great and ancient faith is not only alive but also important, primarily in the context of Chinese life and thought, but not exclusively. Putting it crudely, there is the pantheon of gods and their roles; the role of the priests in maintaining cosmic order; the impact of Taoist ideas on other cultures.

THE TAOIST PANTHEON

Let us start with the first of these. It comes as rather a shock to Westerners who have only read the *Tao Te Ching*, that Taoism has Ten Kings of the Hells for its afterlife, each of which makes the traditional Christian hell look rather second-rate in terms of horrors. The role of the god of wealth in supporting the apparently un-Taoist pursuit of money and fame also strikes the outsider as odd, yet he is one of the most important gods for families and businesses – hence his appearance on just about every Chinese calendar! The

Chinese Taoist pantheon is a fascinating study in applied Taoism and while we can only touch upon the main deities, especially those in South China and the Chinese diaspora, it is worth examining, not least because it is in this form that most Chinese will know and have made use of Taoism.

The Taoist pantheon is an hierarchical one modelled on the Chinese imperial system or, to put it another way, the Chinese imperial system reflected the eternal order. In putting it this way around, we can see the old model of the parallel worlds of the shamanist, but with the idea that the real model, real reality as it were, lies in the spiritual zone.

At the summit of the pantheon, but not of the theological model, stands, or rather usually sits, the Jade Emperor. In saying that he is not at the top of the theological model, I am not trying to confuse you. Taoism has a theological model of a triad which is the summation of the system. This triad has taken many different shapes and forms over the centuries, and to this day is capable of different sets of deities. The two most prevalent ones are the two versions of the Three Pure Ones.

THE THREE PURE ONES

One version of the Three Pure Ones includes The Heavenly Sage of the Original Beginning. This figure is almost a personification of the Tao as the origin; as the point of beginning. He is the *Tao Te Ching*'s One (see Chapter 39 and 42, for example). Next comes the Jade Emperor – in essence the spirit of Tao as it sustains and protects. Finally, we have the Heavenly Sage Jade Dawn of the Golden Gate who has elements of the future and of the Way about him.

However, there is another version of these Three Pure Ones. The Original Beginning remains as the head, for as we have seen this is Tao itself. The second is Lao Tzu as the immanent expression of the Tao. The third (at times confused with the Jade Emperor) is the Yellow Emperor, the model of the perfect human expression of the Tao. When the Yellow Emperor is clearly distinguished from the Jade Emperor, then the Jade Emperor appears below the Three Pure Ones.

The reason I used the term 'theological' earlier was to make the point that in the Three Pure Ones we have a clear schema of origin, manifestation and purpose, which is then articulated through the pantheon. So let us now turn to the pantheon.

THE JADE EMPEROR

The Jade Emperor rules in the highest of the heavens. He is in charge of all existence, both physical and spiritual. However, he is far from being an all-powerful deity. There are many stories which show his will being thwarted or him being shown scant regard. For example, there is the story of his birthday party. When the world was young, the Jade Emperor invited all the animals and creatures of the world to his birthday party. To his great disappointment, only twelve came, the rest could not be bothered! These twelve were rewarded by being made the twelve animals of the Chinese calendar.

Nevertheless, the Jade Emperor does have at his command considerable forces to help him ensure obedience to his will. Key amongst these are his nephew Erh-ling and his doorkeeper Wang. Erh-ling is probably the most powerful of all the Taoist gods in terms of sheer strength and magic. He it is who leads the heavenly troops when the heavenly generals have failed. He is also a superb magician. Even the anti-Taoist book *Monkey* recognizes this in that it is Erh-ling alone who is able to outwit Monkey and capture him. It is perhaps not accidental that Erh-ling's daughter is the one women pray to for a good marriage!

While Erh-ling carries out the Jade Emperor's commands with skill, and when necessary with magic and force, Wang is his faithful messenger. He it is who bears the messages of the Jade Emperor, who summons the spirits and, when necessary, the humans to face the court of Heaven. For this reason, he is often to be found depicted at the gates of Taoist temples.

Within the Court of Heaven, the Jade Emperor presides over a whole bureaucracy of ministries which run the world. These include ministries for Thunder and Wind, Wealth, Literature, War, Exorcisms, various types of illness and so forth. We shall return to some of these later.

THE EARTHLY HIERARCHY

Below these ministries is the hierarchy which resides on Earth and in the waters. Taking the waters first, this is the domain of the Dragon Kings and their hordes. As ancient Chinese geography and cosmology believed that there were four seas, so there are four Dragon Kings. They rule over the waters and all their inhabitants and are not always at peace with Humanity. Indeed, at times the Dragon Kings seek to subdue Humanity and these struggles are only resolved at the Heavenly Court. The story of No-cha (Nez Ha) captures this well. No-cha was a precocious child of one of the emperors who had been taught various skills by an ancient immortal. One day, because of crimes committed by people, the Dragon King of the area demanded a human sacrifice to atone for this disruption of the natural order. However, the Dragon King also used it as an occasion to demand servility from the Emperor. No-cha was enraged at this and defied the Dragon King. In the process, No-cha killed the Dragon King's son. The Dragon King arose in all his fury and threatened the Emperor that unless No-cha was handed over to him, he would destroy the entire country. Unwillingly, the Emperor complied with this, and No-cha went sadly but obediently to his death to save the people. However, through the intervention of his old master the immortal, No-cha was reborn as a deity and defeated the Dragon King who had now overstepped the mark. In the end, Heaven decreed that No-cha was in the right and restrained the Dragon Kings.

The Dragon Kings are very jealous of their powers and in particular, guard the isles of immortality. The Emperor Ch'in Shih Huang Ti, whom we have met earlier in the book, is reputed to have died after an encounter with one. He believed that the Dragon Kings were blocking his ships from reaching the Isles of the Blessed. So he marched to the sea shore and declared war on the Dragon King. The Dragon King appeared and Ch'in Shih Huang Ti ordered his archers to fire at him. Wounded, the Dragon King sank back beneath the waves. But the next night the Emperor dreamt that the Dragon King accused him of the assault and by the morning the Emperor was dead.

Leaving the waters, let us come to the hierarchy here on Earth. The head of this hierarchy, echoing many of the powers of the Jade Emperor, is the Great Emperor of the Eastern Peak. The Eastern Peak is the famous T'ai Shan, the most important of the five Taoist holy mountains, and one of the most visited sites in modern China today. The Great Emperor is the deity through whom the Jade Emperor acts on earth. As such he is really of more significance to the ordinary believer than the Jade Emperor, for it is he who ordains when people will be born, when they will die and in what form they will be reborn. Indeed, popular belief has it that all souls arrive and depart from T'ai Shan. The Great Emperor of the Eastern Peak ranks alongside Chang Tao Ling as a popular figure for dealing with evil and bad fortune. With the Thunder god, they offer protection against the forces of evil. Charms signed by the Great Emperor are often to be found in Chinese homes and appear in the Almanac. They open in exactly the way an imperial order would open, 'Listen and obey', and usually end with the imperial order 'Let the Law be obeyed; let this order be respected and executed straightaway'.

Emperor of the Eastern Peak

Under the Great Emperor comes an array of local deities who have responsibility for the areas of the world. These gods are know collectively as the Gods of the Walls and Ditches. They usually rank from a deity of the province down to the local gods in the house. Their role is to oversee and guard the lives of those in their areas and to report to the Jade Emperor and the Great Emperor on a regular basis in order to ensure that the humans are keeping their side of the balance of yin and yang in harmony.

What is fascinating about most of these Gods of the Walls and

117

Ditches is that they are almost all known historical figures, some of whom only died a few hundred years ago. For instance, the god of Peking is Yang Chi-sheng. He was an official under the Ming dynasty and was executed in 1556 after trying to defend the people against over taxation.

Temple to the Gods of the Walls and Ditches

We have already touched briefly upon the house earth gods and mentioned the role of the kitchen god. These deities, even in places where the system of a full hierarchy of Gods of the Walls and Ditches has collapsed or never been in place, are still held to be of great importance. Two other household or business gods are also important. These are the door gods. These two fierce-looking gentlemen are again based upon historical personages and upon a true story.

The T'ang Emperor T'ai-tsung (AD 626–649) was awoken one night by evil spirits creating havoc in and around his bedroom. Terrified that they would return, the Emperor found it increasingly difficult to sleep – and indeed they would return spasmodically. The Emperor grew seriously ill and drew near to death. In desperation, two of his generals, Ch'in Shu-pao and Hu Ching-te offered to stand guard outside his room to frighten away the evil spirits. This they did for many nights until the evil spirits had given up and left. The Emperor now became concerned about the two generals and their lack of sleep. So, to ensure that the demons never returned and that his generals got their sleep, he ordered paintings of them to be posted outside his bedroom. From this is derived the very common practice of having pictures of two fierce, fully armed door gods posted on to the outside of doors in temples, homes and business premises.

There are four other major deities which we need to meet in this whirlwind tour through the celestial realms on earth before we turn to the underworld. The first of these is the god of wealth, Ts'ai Shen. He is easily recognized because he is to be seen everywhere from bank statements to home shrines. He is dressed as a high-ranking mandarin and carries a scroll with his name on it. He is especially favoured at Chinese New Year when it is hoped that he will provide a wealthy and successful year ahead. Like the kitchen god, his statue is often renewed annually and cardboard statues of him are to be found on sale just about everywhere around New Year. He it is who can bestow good fortune upon an individual or enterprise and many are the prayers offered to him.

The second deity, who is not as powerful now as he used to be, but is still important, is the god of literature. It is perhaps a sign of how seriously the Chinese take their written culture and education that such a deity exists. He it is who can guide the destiny of the academic members of the family. In the old imperial days, he was the god whose aid was sought by candidates for the imperial examination system. Now he is likely to be found in a scholar's study or sitting on the edge of a student's desk at home.

Next we come to one of the most popular of all the deities. The god of war, Kuan Ti, worshipped in places as diverse as the temple, the director's office and the kung fu hall. For Kuan Ti is not just the

119

god of war but of the right use of strength to achieve a desirable and morally justifiable goal. His life story is a fascinating example of how a human being can become a god in Taoism.

Kuan Ti was a soldier called Kuang Chung who lived in the Shansi province during the last days of the Late Han and the first days of the Three Kingdoms (c180–225 AD). Ironically, it was because of the Taoist-inspired Yellow Turbans revolt that Kuang Chung first took up arms. He and two companions vowed to fight to restore order, to overcome the Yellow Turban rebels and to help the poor. Murdered by treachery around AD 220–225, he was soon a major figure in folk tales – a sort of Robin Hood and King Arthur mixed together. Over the centuries his role began to change and he became an object of devotion. In AD 1120 he was posthumously made a Duke. In 1128, he was upgraded to Prince. During the fourteenth century he was given the title Warrior Prince and Bringer of Civilization. Finally, in 1594 he was made a god and given the title of Faithful and Loyal Deity (Ti means deity), Supporter of Heaven and Protector of the Realm. Thus was Kuang Chung transformed into Kuan Ti and, together with his two companions, he is worshipped and invoked to this day.

Finally we have the Empress of Heaven, who is <u>not</u> the wife of the Jade Emperor but a goddess of the seas. Again, an historical person, she gained her place because of the efficacy of prayer to her and because she intervened to save national navies or imperial princes from death at sea. She is greatly honoured by the sea people of the coasts of China and as such her cult has also spread overseas.

It now remains for us to look at the Ten Kings of the Hells of Taoism and then the Three Gods of Happiness, Wong Tai Sin and the Immortals.

THE TEN KINGS OF THE HELLS

Taoism has Ten Kings of Hell presided over by King Yama. His portrait is without doubt the most reproduced one in Chinese belief for he is pictured upon all the Bank of Hell notes which are burnt by the million, day after day. The idea is that the Hells are not that dissimilar to bureaucracy here on Earth, in other words they can be bribed. Furthermore, certain comforts can be secured if the dead have money banked up in Hell. Thus at funerals, New Year and Ching Ming, vast amounts of this colourful paper money are burnt to provide the dead with the means to live.

Before proceeding to the various Hells, it may just be worth giving some of the punishments you will encounter. You may be flayed alive; buried in vermin; gnawed by animals; tied to a heated pillar; laid on a fiery bed; buried under wooden pillars; ripped open, minced up and thrown to dogs, and so on. Be under no illusion, the Taoist Hell is a place quite as fearful as anything the West could invent – if not more so.

Each of the Hells is ruled by a king who is the head judge. So in the first Hell sits King Ch'in-kuang. He judges the souls immediately upon their entry into Hell. Any who are without fault are immediately sent back to earth in their new form. The rest begin their slow and dreadful journey through Hell. The first encounter they have is with the Mirror of the Wicked. Here, face after face appears to accuse the dead person. These are the souls of all of those, animal as well as human, which the person killed during his or her life on earth. Any person who committed suicide is also sent back to earth by King Ch'in-kuang, for in taking their own lives they have tried to force the hand of Heaven. Thus they must be returned, albeit as ghosts, to live out the remainder of their years as allocated by Heaven. This king is also the one who has a special place kept for all the monks who have neglected their prayers. They are kept in darkness until they have recited all the prayers they forgot – an interesting comment on monastic life!

The king of the second Hell is Ch'u-chiang. This king has sixteen sub-departments within his Hell and he has special responsibility for the following categories: marriage brokers who are dishonest; bad doctors; those who have harmed animals or humans.

The ruler of the third Hell is Sung-ti who punishes lying officials, bad-tempered women and slaves who disobey – in other words those who step out of line in the Confucian influenced mould of filial piety and obedience.

King Wu-Kuan presides over the fourth Hell where people who are mean, swindlers or deceivers go.

The fifth Hell is ruled by King Yama and here come those who have broken religious laws and codes of morality. It is also the place where those associated with prostitution come. It has a specially terrible punishment by which the dead are made to watch what has happened to their loved ones back in the world of the living. They watch as the disasters and misfortunes initiated by their evil

121

behaviour unfold. After this they then go through the usual list of terrors.

The sixth Hell has King Pien-ch'eng. Here are those who have abused the names, images or powers of the gods, the temples or the faiths.

The seventh king is T'ai-shan Chun. To this Hell come those who destroy tombs, engage in cannibalism or who maltreat their servants.

The eighth Hell, ruled by King P'ing-teng is reserved for those who lack filial piety, especially for sons who rebel against their parents.

The ninth Hell is ruled by King Tu-shih which is the most terrible place of all. For it is here that those who commit suicide and who cannot work off their remaining years are sent. They are cast into the City of the Suicides from whence there is no escape and they have to relive their suicide time and time again. Others who come to this Hell include people such as abortionists, and writers and readers of obscene literature.

The tenth king of Hell doesn't actually have a Hell as such. He is King Chuan-lun, the king in charge of the wheel of rebirth. He it is who decides what form the rebirth should take. The soul about to be reborn is given a soup-like drink which makes it forget about its previous life and the tortures of Hell.

There are not many temples where the full Ten Kings of Hell are given their own shrine rooms, nor even statues, but they are often depicted upon banners and wall paintings which hang in the Taoist temples. At special festivals, such as the Hungry Ghost Festival, these are brought out and displayed. The Hungry Ghost Festival takes place roughly once every ten years. Vast outdoor shrines and temples are built and here offerings of food and money are brought to ensure that any ghosts who do not have families to look after them can receive enough food and money to make their way through the Hells. If they do not have this, they will haunt the area and cause trouble. The Hungry Ghost Festival is a very popular one and greatly supported.

Finally we need to just look at the Three Gods of Happiness, Wong Tai Sin and the immortals.

THE THREE GODS OF HAPPINESS

In almost every Chinese home, workplace, restaurant and place of leisure or entertainment, you will find the three figures of the Three

Gods of Happiness. These three are easily recognized. The oddest looking is also usually the shortest. He is a bald man with a huge head, who carries an old gnarled stick and a large peach. He is the god of longevity and looks the part! If he is seated, it is on a crane, another symbol of long life. Beside him will be the god of happiness who is dressed like a very high ranking official, and the god of success, who is a benign-looking gentleman in civilian clothes. These three are reputed to be able to bestow great happiness on those who worship properly and their ubiquity seems to indicate that many people have high hopes of them!

Three Gods of Happiness

WONG TAI SIN

Aside from these major gods, each area will have its own special deity who, for a variety of reasons, will have become very popular. A good example of this is the deity who is most popular in Hong Kong, Wong Tai Sin. The vast and beautiful temple of Wong Tai

Sin in Kowloon bears witness to his fame and reputation for power. The core of the temple worship is divination by means of shaking a bamboo container filled with a hundred numbered sticks. When a number falls out as you shake it, this is your fortune reading. The sayings of Wong Tai Sin are very similar in style to those of the *I Ching* and their interpretation often reads like a cross between the commentaries on the lines of the *I Ching* and parts of the *Tao Te Ching*. One of these was given in the first chapter.

The worship of Wong Tai Sin in Hong Kong began in 1915 when a father and son brought a painting of the deity from near Canton. Originally installed in a small temple on Hong Kong island, it moved to Kowloon in 1921. Originally the temple was only for the use of members of a special society, but since 1956 it has been open to all and has rapidly become one of the most popular temples. It is very typical of the normal Taoist temple in that, away from the shrine dedicated to Wong Tai Sin in the main hall, there are smaller halls with shrines dedicated to Confucius and the Buddha. The following is a translation of his autobiography as passed down generation after generation.

'As a young shepherd boy I spent my early childhood at Kim Hwa Mountain located at the north of Kim Hwa City in Chekiang Province . . . Orientated at the north of Kim Hwa Mountain was the Hill of Red Pines where I took abode. This hill, densely forested and often hidden in clouds and fog, was seldom visited by outsiders. . . .

My childhood was marred by poverty and hunger compelling me to start earning my daily bread as a shepherd boy at the age of five. At fifteen I was fortunate enough to have been blessed by a fairy who led me to a stone cave where I learned the art of refining cinnabar nine times into an immortal drug. For forty years in succession I lived in seclusion from the rest of the world until my brother broke this isolation. His early efforts were at first futile. However, through the guidance of a fortune-teller he located me. My brother queried me of the whereabouts of the sheep under my custody. To this I replied that they could be traced in the east of Kim Hwa Mountain. He was surprised on arrival to find nothing but heaps of white boulders which quickly transformed into sheep at my call. Fascinated by this

impressive show of mine, my brother also took steps to learn to become an immortal.'
(From a paper prepared by the Sik Sik Yuen Secretariat, January 1983.)

Here is a perfect example of how popular Taoism interacts with the concept of the reclusive sage, ending in a devotional shrine where reclusiveness and non-action are the last things on people's minds. On the Eight Immortals, I need say very little. We have met them earlier (pages 102–7). All that needs stressing is that they are very important to people today, both as stories and as deities. Their quasi-anarchic behaviour; their favouring of the poor and the oppressed over the wealthy and powerful and their humour and mocking of convention is a salutory reminder that Taoism has always had a subversive and political dimension to it, which is ignored by anyone at their peril. What the Immortals tell us is, laugh at pretension; care for the poor and watch out for the pious!

COSMIC RENEWAL

Having looked at the pantheon of gods, albeit only in the barest outline, let us look at the second area of the continuing impact of Taoism. This is in the area of cosmic renewal and harmony. Because of the focus on the philosophical dimensions of Taoism, the West has paid little attention to what could be described as the Liturgies of the Cosmos of Taoism. At a time when people are rediscovering the old aboriginal traditions in places such as Australia and South America, with their ideas of ritual and cosmic well-being, it is perhaps surprising that the vast, beautiful and thought-provoking liturgies of the Taoists have not been more explored by the West. It is no exaggeration to say that the main function of Taoist priests today is that of ensuring the continued cycle of cosmic renewal liturgies. These try to make sure that the balance of yin and yang, the interaction between Heaven, Earth and Humanity, and the eternal struggle between order and chaos are kept going along the lines of the Way. While extraordinarily complex, these liturgies and rites carry a basic message about the relationship between human beings and the rest of creation, both spiritual and material. The message is that the role we have to play is that of tending the balance and maintaining the harmony. If we fail to do this, then chaos and disorder break out on the Earth and the world as we know it will collapse. It is within these vast, cosmic, liturgical and ritualistic roles that Humanity finds its true destiny according to Taoism. It is also within this context that much of what we have already discussed earlier in this chapter derives its ultimate meaning and purpose.

In the chapter on the development of Taoist schools between the second and tenth centuries AD, we encountered various traditions of liturgy and cosmic renewal. Virtually all of the major schools are still flourishing in one form or another today and their liturgies are enacted year in and year out. The schools are still as fiercely disparaging of each other as they were a thousand years ago, even though a great deal of borrowing has taken place. To the lay Taoist, this does not matter. He or she knows that through the enacting of the rituals and magic, they can participate in the cosmic world and help the dead to rebirth or to release, maintain the well-being of their family or overcome evil forces. To the Taoist priest, what he is doing is nothing more or less than fine-tuning the cosmos according to the Way of Tao.

The idea that through liturgy a correct attitude towards the world can be maintained and nourished is not unique to Taoism. From Australian Aborigines to the Greek Orthodox Church the same idea pertains in different forms. There is not enough time or space here to elaborate on these Taoist rituals for they are very long and complex, but perhaps one example will help. This is the ritual of Returning to the Unity.

In Chapter 42 of the *Tao Te Ching* there are the famous lines which outline fundamental Taoist cosmology:

> Tao gives birth to the One;
> The One gives birth to the two;
> The two give birth to the three;
> The three give birth to all things.

In the ritual of Returning to the Unity, the Taoist priest travels backwards in this formula, starting from the reality of the existence of all things. By a complex process of refinement, he moves from the knowledge of and experience of all things to their roots in the three. The Three here is taken to be the Three Pure Ones, the forms of the realities of the Tao as Original Beginning, Lao Tzu and either the Jade Emperor or the Gate of the Jade Dawn. As Taoism teaches that the human body is a microcosm of the universe, these three deities

126

can be found within the body by the process of meditation and ritual. They reside in the lower abdomen. The Three is also believed to refer to the three principles of existence, namely breath, spirit and the vital essence. From these arise the five elements – wood, fire, earth, metal and water – which constitute all living things.

From the Three the priest moves back to the Two. The two are Heaven and Earth, though some say also yin and yang. From their interaction come the essences of life – the three. They reside in the centre of the body and can be located by meditation and ritual.

From the Two the priest goes back to the One. The One is the origin of life – breath, ch'i. This is what moves all things and could be described as being pure energy. The seat of ch'i, of pure energy, is to be found in the head.

Having successfully returned to the successive stages of the cosmology and discovered them within yourself – a process which takes many many years to achieve – the Taoist priest returns to the ultimate root, the Tao itself. In doing so, he has helped both to simplify the cosmos and thus revitalize its parts and to re-emphasize the inter-related nature of the parts, both cosmically and internally. This ritual is not just a personal action of meditation, but a ritual through which reality and the ultimate are integrated and renewed through the priest.

THE CONTINUING INFLUENCE OF TAOISM

Finally, we come to a new area of the continuing influence of Taoism. This stretches way beyond the Chinese world. The images, language and ideas of Taoism, albeit of only a very small part of Taoism, have entered the vocabulary of the West in a most surprising, and often very inaccurate way. The term Tao has been used to describe and or justify a vast array of alternative positions and ideas from the famous Tao of Physics to the Tao of Computer Technology. Much that has been written using the name of Tao, bears little, if any, relation to the living and historic faith as we have explored it. In certain instances, the word Tao has ceased to have any link with the faith and has become instead a term which stands in its own right within the context of western culture. The dilemma for those who are interested in Taoism as a living faith is whether or not this development can be seen as a new dimension of Taoism.

I have to confess that I am in two minds about this. At one level,

I regret that Taoism has been so exploited by 'New Age' writers who wouldn't know a Chinese character if it bit them, and whose knowledge of Taoism is limited to reading a translation of the *Tao Te Ching*. In taking images out of context, the danger is always that what you take is what you find comfortable and reassuring. This is not actually to encounter the faith. Taoism in its various and varied historic, philosophical and practical manifestations, has a great deal to say to our culture of individualism, of power, of dualistic thinking and of materialism, that we need to hear. What it has to say is often painful, challenging and uncomfortable. It also cannot be grasped in a few days or weeks. It calls for study, reflection, meditation, practice, failure and starting again. Taoism is not easy and anyone who claims it is is deluding you. The model of Lieh Tzu spending years and getting nowhere (page 56) should remind us of this.

Thus I regret that Western culture and individuals do not tend to want to spend the time studying the faith and truly tackling its insights. In simply using that which we think we can understand, that which immediately appeals or that which reassures, we are missing out on what could be a truly mind-bending encounter.

However, that said, perhaps what is happening to certain Taoist images and terms, insights and practices is that they are now entering a new manifestation. As such, it will bear little resemblance to the original faith in any of its historic expressions. But it may be that some of the eternal verities and insights which Taoism emphasizes will re-emerge in a way which can help the West. This is, after all, what has happened in religious life time and time again. The Chinese transformation of Buddhism is a classic example. Religion does not survive unless it can adapt. What is important, however, is that faith should both be capable of changing itself and of changing society at the same time. At times the Taoism which is emerging is so emasculated and individualistic as to be meaningless.

I can think of many ways in which we need Taoist insights in our contemporary world. The relationship to the rest of creation which is so powerfully expressed in the cosmic renewal liturgies and in the cosmological models of Taoism can perhaps offer us a new way of appraising our place in nature in the light of the current environmental crisis. The image of yin/yang, once it is grasped that it represents the struggle of two equal yet opposed forces which by their struggle create a tension, may help us in the sphere of conflict resolution. The idea of non-action achieving ends may be a very necessary counterbalance to the personal success model which our culture so frequently elevates. Certainly many find comfort and help in Taoist medicine and physical exercises. What I hope is that the encounter can go deeper and become more profound, both in terms of helping us define those things which we value in our own cultures and faiths and in helping us with Taoist symbols, myths, beliefs and values which our cultures and faiths simply do not know how to handle, do not understand or have never had.

FURTHER
READING

The following books in English offer the interested reader a chance to go deeper into Taoism. Most of them are still in print, albeit often under new imprints.

Carus P. with Suzuki, T. *T'ai Shang Kan Ying P'ien*, Open Court, Chicago, 1906 (reprinted many times since).

DeWoskin, K. J. *Doctors, Diviners, and Magicians of Ancient China: Biographies of Fang-shih*, Columbia University Press, New York, 1983.

Feng, Gia-fu and English, Jane *Tao Te Ching*, Wildwood House, Hampshire, 1973 (often reprinted).

Graham, A. C. *The Book of Lieh-tzu*, Columbia University Press, New York, 1990 edition.

Da Liu, *The Tao and Chinese Culture*, RKP, London, 1981.

Kaltenmark, Max *Lao Tzu and Taoism*, Stanford University Press, Stanford, California, 1969.

Kwok Man Ho, O'Brien, Joanne and Palmer, Martin *The Eight Immortals of Taoism*, Rider, London, 1990.

Lagerwey, John *Taoist Ritual in Chinese Society and History*, Macmillan, New York, 1987.

Legge, James *The Chinese Classics*, reprinted by Southern Materials Center, Taipei, 1983.

Maspero, Henri *Taoism and Chinese Religion*, University of Massachusetts Press, Amherst, 1981.

Munro, Donald *The Concept of Man in Early China*, Stanford University Press, Stanford, California, 1969.

Needham, Joseph *The Grand Titration*, Allen and Unwin, London, 1979.

 Science and Civilisation in China, vols II and III, Cambridge University Press, England, 1956 and 1959.

Palmer, Martin, Kwok Man Ho and O'Brien, Joanne *The Contemporary I Ching*, Rider, London, 1989.

Palmer, Martin *T'ung Shu*, Rider, London, 1986.

Saso, Michael *The Teachings of Taoist Master Chuang*, Yale University Press, New Haven, 1978.

Waley, Arthur *The Nine Songs*, Allen and Unwin, London, 1955. *The Way and its Power*, Grove Press, New York, 1958.

Watson, Burton *The Complete Works of Chuang Tzu*, Columbia University Press, New York, 1968.

Welch, Holmes and Seidel, Anna *Facets of Taoism*, Yale University Press, New Haven, 1979.

Welch, Holmes *The Parting of the Way*, Methuen, London, 1957.

INDEX